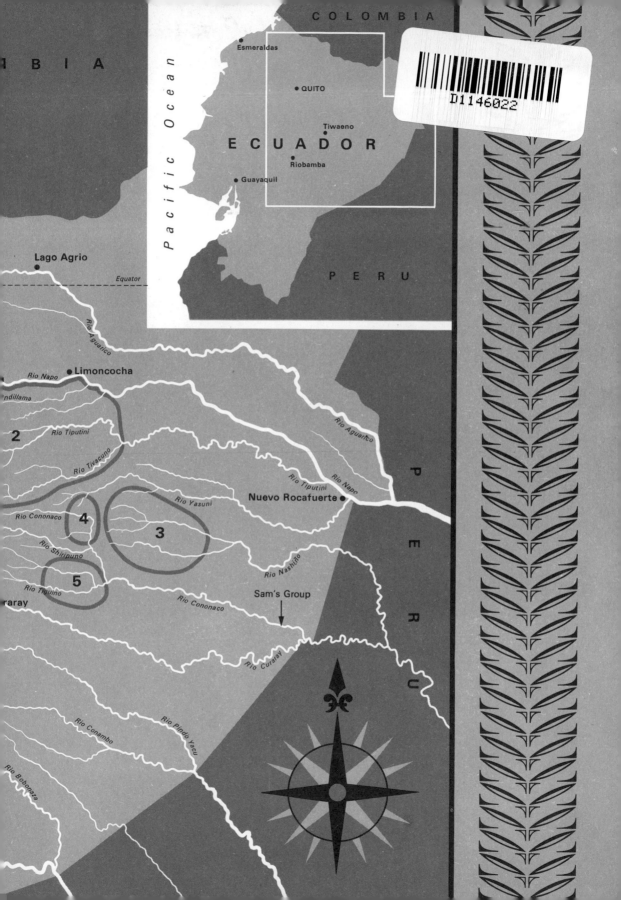

COLOMBIA

Esmeraldas

• QUITO

Tiwaeno

E C U A D O R

• Riobamba

• Guayaquil

Pacific Ocean

Lago Agrio

Equator

Rio Aguarico

Rio Napo   • Limoncocha

ndillama

2

Rio Tiputini

Rio Tivacuno

Rio Aguarico

Rio Tiputini

Rio Napo

Nuevo Rocafuerte

Rio Yasuni

Rio Cononaco

4

3

Rio Shiripuno

Rio Nashiño

5

Rio Tiguino

Rio Cononaco

raray

Sam's Group

P E R U

Rio Curaray

P E R U

Rio Conambo

Rio Pindo Yacu

Rio Bobonaza

A Saint among Savages

ROSEMARY KINGSLAND

A Saint among Savages

Photographs by
JOHN WRIGHT

COLLINS
St James's Place, London
1980

William Collins Sons & Co Ltd
London · Glasgow · Sydney · Auckland
Toronto · Johannesburg

All photographs reproduced in this book are
by John Wright, except for the following:
between pp. 80-81, photographs 1-2 and
pp. 96-97, photograph 1 by Nate Saint;
pp. 80-81, photograph 4 by Malcolm Nurnberg;
pp. 96-97, photograph 2 and pp. 120-121,
photograph 1 & 3 by Elisabeth Elliot; pp. 152-153,
photograph 5 by Cornell Capa.

Endpaper maps by Tom Stalker Miller

First published 1980

ISBN 0 00 216740 9

Made and printed in Great Britain by
William Collins Sons & Co Ltd Glasgow

Contents

John Wright and Rosemary Kingsland wish to thank
Programa de Antropología para el Ecuador, together with the Programme for
New World Anthropology, who very generously assisted logistically and in
all ways. Dr Duncan Pederson of the above Foundation in Quito for his
interest and kindness:
but most of all, Presley Norton, also of the above Foundation – a remarkable
man.

Author's Note

THEIR NEIGHBOURS, THE QUICHUAS, FIRST called them the Aucas, which in the Quichua tongue means Savages, or The Wild Ones.

Of all the Amazon jungle tribes, they seemed to be the most dangerous, savage, and unpredictable. For centuries this Stone Age tribe have held their eleven thousand square miles of virgin forest on the eastern slopes of the Ecuadorian Andes against all intruders, from the Spanish Conquistadores of the sixteenth century to the oil men of today, using their spears with deadly accuracy before fading back into their jungle stronghold. They were, truly, The Wild Ones.

But to them, this name is an insult. With splendid assurance, they call themselves *Wagrani* – 'We, The People'.

They are The People, and their land is The Land. For them, there is no world beyond.

Although the rest of the world today calls them the Aucas, in this book they are also called by their own name, Wagrani.

ROSEMARY KINGSLAND

Preface

I WAS A SCHOOLGIRL IN 1956 and I remember very clearly the day we were told about the massacre of five young American missionaries in the jungles of the Amazon. We felt a special interest, I remember, because my class was studying the work of missionaries as part of a project. For days newspapers and magazines were filled with details of the tragedy and events of an unknown world were forced into people's consciousness. In our cushioned world such things as Stone Age Indians, spears and savage death had little meaning. In time the story was forgotten and my memory of the details with it.

Two years ago I was talking to explorer/photographer John Wright, on his return from a major expedition to the prehistoric Los Tayos caves in southern Ecuador. I was startled when he added: 'And then I went to stay with Rachel Saint, an American woman who has lived with the Auca Indians ever since they killed her brother.'

This brother was Nate Saint – one of the murdered missionaries I had read about as a schoolgirl. I had never known the sequel to his tragic story – that his sister had gone to live for twenty years deep in the Amazon jungle with his killers, members of one of the most dangerous tribes in the world.

I listened, fascinated, as John Wright told me all he knew about Rachel Saint, about Dayuma, the Auca girl who had risked her life by leading Rachel into the tribe and who had remained her closest friend ever since, and about Sam, Dayuma's son whom Rachel had practically adopted.

As the story unfolded, it seemed full of the most amazing coincidences. The teenage Rachel had decided to dedicate herself to God at about the very moment when Dayuma was born in the jungle. At the same time that Rachel started to train as a missionary, Dayuma fled the jungle, escaping from inter-tribal killings, to take refuge on a hacienda on the outside – the first member of her tribe ever to break away from tradition. When Rachel puzzled as to how she could make contact with the Aucas, the unknown people she had been searching for since her teens – without even knowing their name – she found Dayuma, waiting.

The killings of the five missionaries, although tragic, paved the way for Dayuma to return to her tribe with Rachel and Elisabeth Elliot (whose husband, Jim, had been one of the five speared). Elisabeth Elliot left the jungle after two years to care for her young daughter, but Rachel remained on for eighteen years, a lone white woman in a savage environment.

It was a story I felt I had to tell. I wanted to meet Rachel Saint in person. 'Rachel is not well,' John Wright told me. 'Her sight is fading fast and she needs an operation. She is also suffering from the effects of lead poisoning. Doctors have told her that she won't be able to continue much longer.'

Then I heard that Rachel was in America recovering from a series of delicate operations. I flew to America to talk to her. Unwell as she was, this indomitable woman told me: 'I aim to return to Ecuador. I'm not through yet.' I believed her – she is a fighter. She was back in Ecuador within six months, and I left London at once for South America, only to discover that she had not been able to return to the jungle. But still she wouldn't admit defeat. 'The jungle's my home,' she said. 'I'll be going back.'

In Quito, Ecuador's capital, I met Dayuma's son, Sam. A product of the jungle but educated at an American college, he is a mixture of the past and the future; partly wild and free, partly civilized and tamed. He is a fascinating young man who could well have a vital role to play as a representative of all interests between those who see development of the Amazon Basin as inevitable and those who think it should be preserved, untouched, for all time.

Finally, I met Dayuma, and immediately felt I was in the presence of a very special person. She is serene. Her eyes are warm and wise. What force led her to flee the jungle as a child, and who directed her to return after so many years? These are questions one is forced to ask.

While researching the book I realized that a great deal of controversy surrounded nearly all the subjects covered. It was a controversy for which there was no right or wrong answer: everything was a matter of opinion and everyone was convinced that their beliefs were the right ones. For example, opinion is widely divided over the right of missionaries to work with primitive groups, while missionaries themselves sincerely believe it is their duty to work in these fields. While I have touched on all these conflicts of opinion in writing this book, I have tried not to get too personally involved and I have attempted to write the story in as unbiased a way as possible in order that the reader may draw his or her own conclusion. It was not my intention to write a political book, but to tell in as straightforward a way as possible the story of three people.

Three very different people: Rachel Saint, Dayuma and Sam. Why and for what purpose do these three stand out against the tapestry of the Amazon, one of the last wild frontiers left in this world?

This is their story. Perhaps the telling of it will show a deeper design in that tapestry.

ROSEMARY KINGSLAND
London
September 1979

Some of the People Mentioned in the Book

Aentyaeri – initiated a major period of mass spearing
Aepi – captured Quichuan girl who fled jungle with Dayuma
Aka – one of Moipa's wives
Akawo – Dayuma's mother
Amoncawa – first Wagrani to die of polio
Loretta Anderson – one of Rachel's partners in Peru
Rolf Blomberg – Swedish writer who met Dayuma in 1949
Christina Bonnick – Sam's English girl-friend
Caento – (sometimes spelt Tyaento) Dayuma's father and Sam's Wagrani
    name
David Cooper – American missionary, compiled short Wagrani word list in
    1949
Louis Cox – one of Rachel's partners in Peru
Dai – Gimari and Naenkiwi's son
Dayuma – Dayuma's shot grandmother, a family name
'Delilah' – name given to Gimari by five murdered missionaries
Dyuwi – Dayuma's cousin, one of 'Palm Beach' killers
Jim Elliot – one of five murdered missionaries
Elisabeth Elliot – Jim Elliot's wife, who lived with Rachel for two years in
    Tiwaeno
Enea – Dayuma's step-sister, a polio victim
Eunie – Dayuma's blind daughter who drowned
Eva – Dayuma's daughter, Sam's half-sister
Pete Fleming – one of five murdered missionaries

15

Capt. William Flores – jungle pilot friend of Sam

'George' – name given to Naenkiwi by five murdered missionaries, and one of their killers. Husband of Gimari. Killed by Dyuwi

Gikita – Dayuma's uncle, Komi's father, one of 'Palm Beach' killers

Gimari – 'Delilah' – Dayuma's younger sister, who lured five missionaries to their death

Sra Holenbick – Quitan woman with whom Sam lodged while at school

Ignacio – Sam's first given name

Iniwa – half-brother to Amoncawa, died mysteriously

Don Johnson – Director of SIL in Ecuador, Rachel's immediate superior

Karae – Dayuma's grandfather, Akawo's father, a witch doctor, murdered by Moipa

Patricia Kelly – Rachel's replacement in the Auca Protectorate

Komi – Dayuma's husband, son of her uncle Gikita, Sam's step-father

Kimo – one of 'Palm Beach' killers, relative of Dayuma

Kiwa – Dayuma's uncle, Akawo's brother, speared by Moipa

Maengamo – Dayuma's aunt who left the jungle in search of her and met Elisabeth Elliot

Ed McCully – one of five murdered missionaries

Marilou McCully – wife of Ed McCully

Miñimo – Naenkiwi's sister

Mintaka – Dayuma's aunt who left the jungle with Maengamo

Moipa – notorious Wagrani killer, speared Dayuma's father, grandfather and sister, Nimu; himself speared by Downriver group

Nampa – Dayuma's younger brother – some doubt as to his way of death

Nancy 'Hummingbird' – Dayuma's eldest daughter, Sam's half-sister

Natani – Dayuma's aunt

Nimonga – one of Dayuma's cousins, one of 'Palm Beach' killers, died of polio

Nimu – Rachel's Wagrani name; Dayuma's younger sister, speared by Moipa

Olimpia – Miguel Padilla's aunt (Sam's adopted great-aunt)

Omiñia – Dayuma's step-grandmother

Onaenga – Dayuma's younger sister, died in a storm

Miguel Padilla – Dayuma's first (Quichuan) husband, died of measles

Sam Padilla – see Sam

Catherine Peeke – Rachel's first language partner with Dayuma, gained Ph.D. for work on Wagrani grammar

Piyamo – witch doctor blamed for polio epidemic, himself a victim

Katherine Proctor – Rachel's mother

Rachel (Saint) – Wagrani name, Nimu; born in Philadelphia 1914
Lawrence Saint – Rachel's father
Marj Saint – wife of Rachel's youngest brother, Nate
Nate Saint – Rachel's youngest brother, one of five murdered missionaries
Phil Saint – Rachel's brother, a missionary in Venezuela
Rachel Saint – see Rachel
Sam Saint – Rachel's oldest brother, introduced Nate to flying
Sam Caento Padilla – Dayuma's son, born 1951
Mary Sargent – Rachel's second language partner, worked with Dayuma
Don Carlos Sevilla – *patrón* of hacienda where Dayuma fled and where Sam
    was born
Vicente Sevilla – Sam's natural father
Solomon – Dayuma's youngest son, Sam's half-brother
Tariri – chief of head-hunting Shapras tribe in Peru where Rachel worked
    before living with Wagrani
Tidonca – Rachel's first challenge in Tiwaeno
Toña – first Wagrani missionary, killed by Wepe's Ridge group
Glen Turner – Director of Indian Affairs, SIL Quito
Cameron Townsend – founder of SIL, WBT and JAARS
Umi – Dayuma's cousin who fled jungle with her
Wato – Toña's wife, parents killed by Downriver group
Wawae – Dayuma's favourite brother, speared to death
Wepe – notorious Ridge killer
Wiñaemi – Dayuma's cousin who fled jungle with her
Roger Youderain – one of five murdered missionaries
Záparo – a jungle tribe – an old woman is the last surviving member

Abbreviations

SIL – Summer Institute of Linguistics, organization founded by Cameron
    Townsend, affiliated to WBT
WBT – Wycliffe Bible Translators, missionary organization, based in Cali-
    fornia, founded by Cameron Townsend
MAF – Missionary Aviation Fellowship, offering air support to all mission-
    aries
JAARS – Jungle Aviation and Radio Service, organization founded by
    Cameron Townsend to support SIL and WBT missionaries in the field

1

Rachel's Parents – Katherine Proctor and Lawrence Saint

THE GIRLS AT WELLESLEY KNEW that Katherine Proctor was different from them the day she threw her whalebone corsets out of the window.

They watched the fiery débutante from one of Philadelphia's wealthiest families with interest as she plunged into a round of campus revolutionary activities, which, in 1908, for a well-bred female meant enjoying the freedom in public of a natural waistline, skipping church and taking an interest in the arts.

Katherine wrote poetry, dabbled in oils, stayed out as late as she dared, and half the young men from Boston's most exclusive families promptly fell in love with her sparkling grey eyes, her oval face and mass of golden hair.

She must have been doing something really sensational when an elderly gentleman felt forced to gaze at her piercingly on a streetcar and ask, 'Young lady, are you a Christian?'

Katherine was indignant. 'Yes!' she replied, and promptly forgot to go to church on yet another Sunday.

Delicious silk dresses and matching parasols looked twice as delicious on the green banks at a riverside picnic than displayed in the dim interior of a church. After one such picnic on the Wellesley River, punting in the languid waters and eating ripe cherries that, one admirer wrote in a poem, exactly matched her mouth, Katherine returned to discover a note under her study door.

'I came to you for help, but you were out,' was all that was written above the hastily scrawled signature.

Katherine was stunned to discover that at the precise moment she was flirting outrageously in a drifting punt, her class-mate was busy drowning herself in the same waters. The tragedy affected her very deeply, and she began to think more carefully about her way of life and about the Quaker family back at home in Philadelphia who had imposed certain standards which she had been wilfully abandoning.

By the time she returned home after graduating, Katherine knew that somehow she had to make up for failing her friend so badly; for not even guessing how much she was needed, or how intensely miserable the girl had been.

Home was an almost palatial mansion in Wyncote, Pennsylvania, not far from Philadelphia. The park-like grounds were immaculate, the lawns manicured by a sombre Italian immigrant, and the long chicken houses that provided fresh, wholesome eggs – 'we know *precisely* what goes into every one' – were scrubbed out daily. Every piece of equipment inside, and outside, the house was boldly branded with the words, *Josiah K. Proctor*.

Josiah K. Proctor possessed a docile wife and two lovely daughters, Jane and Katherine, although it is not known whether they, too, were branded other than with his initials. He was also described as an inventive genius and had founded the large Proctor and Schwartz Company of Philadelphia on which his solid fortune was based. He was a busy, determined man and lavished a great deal of money but very little attention on his family.

Church on Sunday was one matter that drew his attention, as did the continuing good order of his home and women. The family attended the home Wyncote Presbyterian Church on the day after Katherine's return from College. Ralph Connor, author of *The Sky Pilot*, was the preacher. Suddenly he pointed directly at Katherine, sitting elegantly gloved and hatted next to her parents: 'Young lady, are you doing what God wants you to do?'

The personal appeal, coming so soon after the suicide of her friend, startled Katherine, but at that moment she didn't feel very inspired to do anything about it.

After church, she marched up to Connor and told him that she knew she should be doing something, but had no faith.

Connor nodded: 'But if you are *willing*, you will *know*.'

That same night the young rebel who preferred picnics to church found herself on her knees in her room. Her prayer was short.

'Oh God, I am willing to be shown. I want to know.'

At that moment that mysterious quality known as 'Faith' flooded over Katherine and for the rest of her life she seemed to have steel in her backbone. The same quality that once made her refuse to wear whalebone corsets because she believed they were not good for her now made her refuse to do anything her heart desired if she decided it was not right.

In the morning Katherine went to an Italian mission and arranged to put her education to some use by teaching there instead of enjoying her days in the idle pleasures to which the rich believed their birth entitled them.

She still continued, however, to enjoy some of the benefits of her special position. She called on friends, she rode, she attended exhibitions – and she had an impoverished poet to tutor her at home.

His name was Ezra Pound. It was not long before Katherine was madly in love with the young man who was destined to become one of the great poets of this century. They discussed marriage and were swept into the sublime heights that only two poets in love can know. Katherine thought Ezra all but perfect. He only needed to change one or two of his rather bohemian ways, to attend church with her, and perhaps to teach at the Mission . . .

Ezra was stubborn. Katherine, of course, could do as many Good Works as she wished, and had the money to perform, but nothing in the world, or in heaven, if there were such a place, was going to change him. Katherine was stubborn, too. They would break off their relationship; she would learn to forget him.

'Much as I love you,' she told the bewildered poet, 'I love the Lord more.'

Ezra Pound and Katherine parted, and lost touch with each other. They met again over thirty years later when he was locked up in a mental asylum after being found guilty of being a traitor to the United States. Katherine visited him with one of her sons, and told him that if he had listened to her all those years earlier perhaps things would have been different. It is not recorded what he replied, but there is little doubt that as she looked at him, Katherine must have been thinking of the extraordinary twist of fate that had introduced the poet, Hilda Doolittle, into his life.

After his love affair with Katherine broke up, Ezra went to live in Italy, and it was there, during the Second World War, that he became involved in the activities that led to his eventual arrest. At his trial he pleaded insanity and so escaped the electric chair. It was during his Italian adventure that Hilda Doolittle became his lover.

At the same time as Katherine was in love with Ezra Pound, an impoverished young artist called Lawrence Saint was in love with Hilda Doolittle. While Katherine was telling Ezra that she couldn't love him because he could not love God, Lawrence Saint was repeating almost the same conversation to the astonished Hilda Doolittle who couldn't see what God had to do with it.

*

A Saint among Savages

At the confluence of the Susquehanna and the Monongahela rivers, the town of Pittsburgh sprang up to service the hooting river boats, the buckskinned cowboys and the big herds. It was a rough, wild, pioneer town. Among the roughest and richest was James Saint, who cared nothing for art and a great deal about business, which was unfortunate, since his son, James, was a talented natural artist.

While he was still a boy, young James would draw everything and everyone, on anything, anywhere. Sawdust on a wall, mud in the street, steam on a window, all got the rapt attention of his magic touch. He was so good that a travelling businessman offered to send the young genius to Paris, for a formal art education. James junior soon put him right. His own father could afford to pay, but wouldn't, so James guessed he would just muddle on, teaching himself.

He guessed correctly. He did muddle on, teaching himself, and by the time he was old enough to earn his own living he was a master of landscape, frontier scenes and portraits – and his hard-headed father had cut him off.

James A. Saint quickly discovered that although he could imitate a Corot or a Rembrandt with equal facility, he couldn't sell oils. What he could sell were the then highly fashionable silhouettes, and he travelled the old-time fairs and expositions where he set up his booth which declared 'Your Face Cut without Pain!'

His sharp little scissors moved over the black paper like lightning, but all that filled his pockets were dimes and cents and those not too regularly. For all that, he was content, and in time married and produced a family of two sons, James and Lawrence, and a daughter, Hazel.

By the time Lawrence was a youth he was earning his living selling newspapers in the street and had moved to Philadelphia.

Katherine Proctor, in her mansion, and Lawrence Saint, literally in his garret, may have seen each other. She could have passed in her father's fine carriage, and casually looked at the young man selling papers, but they certainly didn't meet on a social level.

Lawrence wanted to be an artist, but a major drawback to this ambition was that he had principles. These principles threatened to come between him and a longed-for travelling scholarship to Europe. Part of his exhibition had to contain a female nude.

Failing all else, Lawrence decided to pray about it. He said it was neither coincidence, nor deference to the brilliance of the rest of his exhibition that made the Academy's governing board waive their ruling. He won the scholarship, travelled to Europe, and discovered what he wanted to do with his life.

He stood in the nave of an ancient cathedral in France, the sun pouring through the breathtaking rose window and flooding, it seemed, his soul with brilliance, and he knew that more than anything, he wanted to revive the lost medieval art of religious stained glass.

On his return to Philadelphia, Lawrence gave up Hilda Doolittle, told his teachers of his decision to study only glass and spent part of his spare time teaching at a small Italian mission in the slum district.

He watched a beautiful, grey-eyed girl with glowing hair and a sweet smile teaching little bootblacks and pickpockets. Her one problem was that the little horrors thought she was far too pretty to keep order. Lawrence came to her rescue and before long became her beau and it wasn't long before Katherine decided that she was going to marry Lawrence. She was a rich heiress and he was a penniless artist with threadbare clothes and few social graces. But he was talented, he was very striking with flaming red hair and his eyes were a beautiful blue. Most important, he had principles. It was enough.

When he went home to western Pennsylvania for the summer vacation, she stored all his paintings in her father's home and when Lawrence returned to the Academy in the fall and won another travelling scholarship to Europe, she firmly declared that she was going with him.

'I refuse to travel alone with any woman who is not my wife,' Lawrence announced. Those principles again!

'Very well, I will become your wife,' Katherine said coolly.

'My father said I should never plan on marrying until I have saved a thousand dollars,' Lawrence said, weakly.

'My aunt has just left me a thousand dollars. Why can't we use that?' Katherine asked radiantly.

Katherine made her own wedding dress and the ceremony was held on 10 June 1910 in the most elegant salon of the Josiah K. Proctor mansion. The room was banked with roses, and those were the buds that Katherine carried. Her hair was dressed in a revived Rennaissance style, curving back in a heart-shape from her calm, broad brow. She looked lovely and Lawrence could not understand why she had chosen him.

'Because he loved God, me, and art – in that order,' Katherine said years later.

Mr and Mrs Lawrence Saint and Mr and Mrs Josiah K. Proctor travelled to Europe together. The Proctors were going to Oberammergau and they paid for the honeymoon trip, although they left the newly-weds in France.

The new bride spent her honeymoon scaling scaffoldings and medieval-style wooden ladders in the soaring interiors of medieval cathedrals, holding her husband's materials while he copied the priceless beauty of the stained-glass windows.

He filled portfolio after portfolio; the complete collection is now held by the Victoria and Albert Museum in London and his book, based on the work of his honeymoon trip, *Stained Glass of the Middle Ages*, has been the standard work in that field for nearly seventy years.

They were ecstatically happy and Lawrence proved that his antipathy for the female nude did not extend to all members of that species, for Katherine very quickly started to produce babies.

There was Sam who became an airline pilot, Phil who became a missionary in Argentina – and, in 1914, Rachel.

Soon there were five more babies including Nate, who was born in 1924; but Rachel was to be the only girl.

2

Rachel's Childhood in the United States

THE BOYS CALLED THEIR TEARAWAY SISTER 'Boochel and Company
Witchazel', although to this day none of them can explain why.

Her Proctor grandparents and all the dowagers of Philadelphia adored her.
Her brothers could not understand it.

True, she had the astonishing blue eyes of their father – 'heavenly blue' as
the exact shade was sometimes sentimentally described; and true, she had the
vivid pink and gold colouring of their mother. But she was still a little cat who
had the face of an angel and the spirit of an unheavenly imp.

She was always getting them into trouble with no effort at all. It was not
so much that Rachel did things for which they were blamed; she did, but it
was more a matter of the fact that they were all furiously jealous of her charm.
Sweetness and light, as they put it. Whatever Rachel did was right and whatever
they did was wrong, it seemed. Rachel was not too perturbed by their natural
brotherly antagonism. She was frequently asked to stay with this friend or
that friend, and when things got really tough at home, she would streak up the
back stairs of their house and lock herself in the bathroom.

As she pointed out to the boys, they could not complain. Their own home
was so scuffed, so many windows were broken, and they were everywhere,
shinning up drainpipes and climbing in and out of windows, whooping with
energy, that it was hardly surprising that they were rarely asked into the stately
Proctor mansion. When they had been invited, she smugly continued, they
had taken over the drawing-room with its highly polished floors and Persian
rugs. They had torn at a wild gallop across the floor, sliding on the rare carpets

25

to bounce furiously on a velvet-covered davenport – finally to catapult through the bay windows of the Georgian front on to a vast pile of feather cushions, stolen from all sources and heaped on the porticoed porch, right in front of the house in full view of any visitor.

And what was more, Rachel maliciously continued while her brothers glowered at her, they were all whooping and screaming like wild savages at the precise moment when their Proctor grandmother had sailed like a galleon in through the door.

Rachel did not think very much of 'savages'. Nor it seemed, did their Proctor grandmother. It was many months before the boys were invited to set foot over the threshhold again.

The situation was, in a way, remarkable. The wild Saint brood lived in a cottage built for them in the very grounds of the mansion from which they were banned.

It was not that the children lacked discipline. Katherine had studied child psychology at Wellesley, and her guide was a book called *How to Reason with a Small Child*, which she looked through in some confusion. Lawrence took as *his* guide the King James version of the Bible, Proverbs 23, verses thirteen and fourteen. 'Withhold not correction from a child: for if thou beatest him with the rod he shall not die. Thou shalt beat him with the rod and shalt save his soul from hell.'

It is not known what Katherine's book had to say about corporal punishment. Whatever it was it was not worded in strong enough language. She had soon tossed her psychology over her shoulder and was wielding her rod with energy when Lawrence was not around.

When they weren't being beaten, the boys were patted affectionately on the head, and it was a loving, happy household.

By the time six children had arrived in the small cottage, Josiah Proctor had died, and for some reason never discovered by his daughter Katherine, there was no money left to help out when Lawrence's work wasn't going too well.

The Saint family moved from Wyncote to Huntingdon Valley in 1918. The town was more like a village with one main street, two side streets, a general store, a barber's shop and a bank. There may have been more, but Rachel does not remember.

For her the countryside was the next best thing to Paradise.

She knew a great deal about Paradise, although she was so young. The whole family trooped to church, like an orphanage on the move, every Sunday morning, and to various evangelistic meetings every Sunday evening. Before lunch, the children went to Sunday school, and after tea they were packed off to Christian Endeavour.

Most children would have been exhausted after such a timetable, but to Lawrence Sunday afternoons were a problem.

He had decided that Sunday was a holy day and not a holiday and had to be filled accordingly. After lunch if the weather was fine he usually took his tribe on as sedate a walk as he could make it. They skipped flat stones over the water in Pennypack Creek, they clambered, like acrobats, on high fence rails, they ate oxheart cherries and wild strawberries, and sometimes they broke away and chased cottontail rabbits. They said they loved these 'calm' Sunday afternoon walks.

If it rained, they all crowded into the large, low parlour, while Katherine took her one day a week off from patching ragged clothes, and Lawrence taught them to paint, using Bible stories as his guide.

Rachel enjoyed drawing but she never became good at it. Best of all she just liked to watch her father. In those days he rarely drew at all, unless it was to sketch a design for his stained-glass windows, so, for her, the Sunday rain sessions were a special treat.

The Huntingdon Valley countryside was a delight to Rachel who was rapidly becoming more and more of a tomboy. Rolling wheatfields edged deep woods of dark cedar and pine. Pale, spotted buttonwood trunks, delicate willows and grey birch stood out.

During the week in the long, hot summers, the children swam in the deep hole in Pennypack Creek; in the winter the dangers were increased as they skated the length of the twisting creek, from the dam at the waterworks to the rapids by the old mill, where the ice was always half melted. They often fell into its bone-freezing depths, but none of them ever succeeded in drowning themselves.

During the winter snows, they sledged over the wheat fields' smooth contours, usually on their long-suffering mother's trays, and in the summer, their ski-slope was the nearly perpendicular barn ladder. They used its well-soaped rungs as a chute and clattered from rung to rung on broken barrel staves. Their arms and legs stayed intact, much to everyone's surprise.

Rachel was always being egged on to the most alarming 'dares' by her brothers. As a child she was plump, healthy, with active muscles, and she merely seemed to bounce when tumbling from trees or falling out of haystacks. Even then, she was a survivor. One of her greatest pleasures was being taken for a ride in the antique electric car they had inherited from the regal Philadelphia Proctor household. The black, lumbering monster had heavy lead batteries stowed fore and aft, strapped in place with leather and brass-buckled bands, and its interior was not unlike a funeral parlour, with silken tassels and blinds and cut-glass vases. Lawrence drove the ancient relic from the back seat, where he directed its movements with a bar. It was very simple. The bar was pushed forward to go in that direction, and backward to go in *that* direction. Rachel cannot recall what happened about sudden bends in the road.

She preferred to ride alone, with just her beautiful mother and handsome, red-bearded father, bowing at their neighbours. There weren't too many of those, but those they met were duly impressed and the little girl loved it after the total contempt her brothers had for all her finer feelings. Riding alone was a very rare event. When the car was trundled out of the sagging barn, it was promptly filled to overflowing with all the Saints, and steering with the bar was a perilous business.

The car was nearly wrecked when Sam drove it illegally and forgot that he wasn't rowing a boat on Pennypack Creek. In a panic he reversed into the barn posts and one ancient edifice collapsed upon another ancient institution. Grandfather Josiah K. Proctor would have turned in his grave.

Two neighbouring spinsters were more forthright. They volunteered the dire prediction that Saints or not, the entire, unruly crew would be turned away from the Golden Gates by St Peter himself. It gave these sisters grim satisfaction to watch all the more high-spirited pranks. They ignored the fact that the children had to let off steam in order to survive their strict regime.

Lawrence had built an altar in their small home and there were Bible readings and prayers every day. On several evenings a week too, the family went to cottage prayer meetings where smoky kerosene lamps flickered over family portraits and Bible texts with equal gloom.

The children cannot recall disliking this extreme background. By the age of five each one knew by heart and loved the stories of the Bible.

'They are as fascinating to a child as a fairy story,' Rachel said. 'We had a solid Quaker tradition which gave us a solid foundation. We knew where we were and we still do.'

The solid foundation was to breed three missionaries, one of whom became a martyr, and a home pastor.

Despite the outdoor fun, life was never very easy after they left the security of Philadelphia. At first Lawrence found it difficult to get commissions and the family knew what real hunger was.

With so many growing bodies to feed, even twelve quarts of milk a day and piles of garden vegetables vanished with heartbreaking speed. Katherine did her best, but at times, for days on end, there was nothing but milk from their cow, and peanuts.

Rachel used to play games with her younger brother Nate, who was so much like her and for whom she had a special affection. She would lift him into an overturned chair and tell him he was a monkey she had caught in the jungle and now she was feeding him some delicious nuts through the bars of his cage.

Nuts can only be delicious and such games entertaining for so long, and often the little ones cried with boredom at their unsatisfying diet. There were times when they were practically starving and Katherine nearly wept when she caught Rachel smiling anxiously at the babies as she coaxed them to eat nuts yet again.

The food was not the only thing different in Katherine's life as an artist's wife.

Lawrence filled the Huntingdon cottage with unusual furniture. He made the dining-table from the sides of an old piano and the benches were hewn from lumber-yard logs. As the years passed Katherine's once fashionable Philadelphia frocks were made over and cunningly disguised as breeches and shirts for her growing brood and her eyes were weakened by stitching late into the night by kerosene lamplight long after her family were sleeping.

The old expression 'when poverty walks in through the door, love flies out of the window' didn't apply in that house, despite all the privations. Never once did Katherine regret her decision, which was just as well. Lawrence was very conscious of the fact that he had taken a wealthy girl and made her poor, but he also knew that the meek would inherit the Kingdom of Heaven.

It is a long tradition that artists be poor, but Lawrence was in a worse position than he need have been because he refused to consider reneging on his promise to himself to dedicate his exceptional talent to the craft of religious stained glass. It seemed, too, as if some of the trials of Bunyan's Pilgrim whom he had recently depicted in glass were to be heaped on his shoulders when he became seriously ill.

Lawrence was to be bedridden for seven years, but when he felt up to it he managed to do some work and his family managed to exist.

Lawrence's long illness and many operations had helped turn his flame-red beard nearly snow white. He had taken to trimming it to a Vandyke point, in keeping with its snowy dignity, he said. With the matching, flamboyant moustache he looked distinguished and most people had started calling him 'Dr Saint', to such an extent that he gave up correcting them.

It was his striking appearance that was to help him on the slow road to financial recuperation and some degree of recognition. He was travelling on a train, having recently been able to move in search of commissions for the first time in many years, when a total stranger stopped and politely asked his name and occupation. Lawrence was startled, and more so when the stranger continued,

'Your resemblance to the portraits of Christ is so strong, I had to ask you.'

'My name is Saint,' Lawrence replied, 'and I make stained-glass windows for churches.'

'And my name is Pitcairn,' the stranger said. 'I am building a cathedral. When can you start on my windows?'

Lawrence worked in Raymond Pitcairn's studio for eleven years and the results are the windows in the Bryn Athyn Cathedral of Philadelphia. His next commission was to make windows for the National Cathedral at Mt St Albans in Washington, and for this Lawrence decided that, finally, he would put into practice all his efforts over the years of rediscovering the medieval stained-glass recipes.

Everyone said that the whole project was impossible, but Katherine marched off to libraries armed with her original notes in Old French, collected on her honeymoon trip, and painstakingly translated them. Lawrence was considerably entertained when he read her notes. The shavings from a cow's hoof meant a whole leg thrown casually into the studio yard by the passing butcher. Human hair involved the local barber sweeping his shop with more energy than he had for years. Raw potato, to take the bubbles from the molten glass, was called for. Flamboyant in all things, Lawrence heaved a massive vegetable into the cauldron and the glass boiled and spattered all over.

The children joined in all the fun of the experiments. They had been called into the studio to see a wall of coloured glass – only to discover a sticky pool on the ground. When the formulae began to work they were as excited as Lawrence. He believed in total family involvement in everything. After a year the first window was ready to go to the cathedral in Washington and be set in lead. Lawrence and the family trooped into the studio for a final check, a final admiring look, and saw every piece of glass scattered on the floor. The wax frames had melted in an unusually hot sun. Lawrence wept in despair, but it was Katherine who saw that not one piece of glass had broken; it could all be reset from the careful colour designs.

A fire that completely gutted the studio was more disastrous, and several major pieces were completely shattered – but the beautiful Last Judgement rose window had been removed to the cathedral by Lawrence on the night before the fire broke out.

Distinguished visitors now began to flock to the studio to watch a famous artist at work. Rachel remembers Dr Howard Kelly, one of the three founders of the Johns Hopkins University and Hospital.

After he and his associates had discussed glass, he turned to the eager Saint children and talked to them about his experiments with snakes and insects. As he talked, they were fascinated by a fresh, crisp rose in his buttonhole. Finally they couldn't control their curiosity about its apparently miraculous non-wilting powers on a hot day.

Dr Kelly turned back his lapel and showed them a small, water-filled glass bulb. 'My flower has a secret source of life,' he said. 'And I do too. Christ is mine.'

Even in small things, and in every moment of their daily lives, the Saint children were introduced to and surrounded by a canopy of religion. It was second nature to them to think of God in all things. Of such material are missionaries made.

Grandpa Saint had been a constant visitor to the household of ten during the lean years, and while he did not contribute much in the way of that solid, chewable sustenance called food, he helped enormously by taking the continuous pressure of eight children from their sick father and overworked mother.

The children found him their most romantic and sympathetic relative. He drew them back to the roots of their land with his fabulous stories of early frontier days and they crowded around his knees in the already crowded kitchen and listened, silent for once, as he told them of buckskinned heroes, rustlers, cattle trails and gunfights.

It was from him that they learned of the river boats on the Susquehanna and of the great unknown that lay to the West. He talked of the spirit of adventure and discovery, of the American Indian and his ways, and as Rachel listened, a dream germinated in her that was not to flourish like a green bay tree on the surface of her mind until ten more years had passed.

The Philadelphia relatives and rich dowagers had not forgotten the little girl lost in an unruly army of boys and even after the Saints had moved to Huntingdon, they still wrote benevolent letters of invitation to Katherine requesting that Rachel be sent to them for visits. They also tactfully sent a few dollars spending money for the child so that she was able to accept without depriving the family.

Katherine liked Rachel to go; she was aware that the girl's life was not going to take her to Wellesley, and while she was glad that it would not include punting on the river with frivolous young débutantes, she placed great value on a good education.

Katherine relaxed when Mrs Parmalee of Washington took the teenage girl completely under her wing. Mrs Parmalee was more than just a million-airess in her own right. Her husband was the sponsor of Lawrence's windows in the Mt St Alban's Cathedral, and she herself was cultured, intelligent and had a genuine fondness for Rachel. She confided in Katherine that she intended making Rachel her heir. There were frequent visits and the warmth grew. Mrs Parmalee finally decided that she would take Rachel for the traditional 'coming out' trip to Europe.

Because they had chosen to go in the winter the trip was restricted to a tour of Britain, and it was to be many years before Rachel saw anything of the rest of Europe.

Rachel was seventeen at the time and small things are what stick in her mind now, nearly fifty years later.

In London she ate a complete vegetable dinner – 'vegetable pie with vege-tables'. In the north and in Scotland, in those days before frozen food, vegetables were unobtainable out of season, and by the time the two women arrived back in London, Rachel declared that she felt like a lump of dough and would have had greens for breakfast if the hotel hadn't thought her too eccentric.

She kept a diary of her trip and one of her favourite memories is of the statue of Fatigue in Princes Street, Edinburgh. She wrote a detailed description of the bodies and straining muscles of the four athletic figures and when she returned to Philadelphia she was introduced to the artist. He had not done one single piece of artistic work until he was forty years old, when he felt driven to leave his job as a bank clerk and become a sculptor.

'He found the only way to express himself was not in words, but in clay, so just like that, he dropped everything and took it up. It was a brave decision, but he had great faith in himself and wanted to do what was right for him. That is important in all things,' Rachel said.

She showed him the pages in her diary describing her feelings about his distant piece of work in Edinburgh and he told her that her words moved him more than anything else he had read. It said all he wanted anyone to say on the subject.

Rachel discovered that although she was so young, she also had a great deal of faith in her own decisions.

During her journey home on the great liner, *Aquitania*, she found that she had no affinity with the exotic, empty way of life led by her fellow first-class passengers. She knew that it was wrong for her.

'It was pretty vapid, really.'

She thought a great deal about her father and about his implacable rule of 'principles in all things' and about her tranquil mother who had kept the family together through many years of great hardship, and she knew that enormous wealth would destroy her own integrity. She made up her mind to tell Mrs Parmalee that she could not be her heir, although she did not know what she did want instead. For an untrained girl it was a great jump from being an heiress to being nothing at the age of seventeen.

It was now 1932. England was behind her and her whole life lay before her, but she didn't think about it in those terms. She only knew that she had to break the news to Mrs Parmalee and then go home to tell her parents. She knew they wouldn't attempt to make her change her mind. They had brought her up, with her brothers, to make firm decisions and to believe that anything decided with a pure, open mind was right, even if it did not seem so at the time.

As the liner approached New York, Rachel decided she would go on deck at daybreak to see the Statue of Liberty. She dressed warmly but left her hair loose. She was the only person on the first-class deck in the freezing sea mist and as a wind blew up, shaking her heavy, corn-gold hair over her face, she shivered and prepared to retire.

It was then that Rachel had a vision.

She knew, beyond a doubt, that God had spoken to her. The vision showed her an unknown, brown-skinned tribe, deep in a green jungle.

She knew that one day she would live with those people and teach them as her own parents had taught her. In the middle of the ocean, in a grey dawn, Rachel got down on her knees on the scrubbed deck and closed her eyes as she promised God she would give her whole life to Him.

Somewhere, beyond the seas, was an unknown people. And some day, vowed the seventeen-year-old girl, she would find them.

3

Rachel, the Young Missionary in Training

ALTHOUGH FROM THEN ON Rachel Saint knew that one day she would work with an unknown people, a quarter of a century was to pass before the time was ripe for her to fulfil her destiny. The threads in the Oriente tapestry had to be woven together, but the important thing was that the tapestry *was* being woven and a pattern *was* emerging.

Because she was so young when she made her decision on the *Aquitania* Rachel went to Percy Crawford's evening Bible school at home, while she helped her mother with the large family. When she was old enough, she went to the Philadelphia College of Bible.

She was sure the place where she was intended to go as a young missionary was China, and when she graduated, she applied. Her disappointment when she was turned down due to a weak back was enormous. At the time she could only feel humiliated that a bodily weakness had let her down; later, she interpreted the disease as God's way of showing her that she was attempting to jump the gun. The stage in the Oriente was not yet ready; the cast was not assembled in their correct place in the drama to come.

After graduating from Bible College, she spent twelve years working in the Keswick Colony of Mercy, 'drying out drunks' as she described it. 'Getting them to see that if they accepted the Lord, there would be no need for the prop of alcohol in their lives.'

It was a dramatic experience for a carefully-brought-up young lady. Rachel saw things she had no conception of, and heard language so totally foreign to her vocabulary that, far from shocking her, she had no idea what it meant.

Such refreshing innocence was a great help on the Bowery, or on Skid Row in Harlem. The Second World War was at its height by then, and many young soldiers and sailors, out on the town, must have thought they were seeing an angel instead of pink elephants in the fair-haired girl with her Dutch doll complexion and brilliant blue eyes.

Rachel saw the war out and eventually celebrated her thirty-fifth birthday. She had been patient, but now the time was right, and she knew it. Her years dealing with alcoholics had given her a toughness and sense of humour unusual in a woman of her background. She had learnt to be firm with men, sometimes in perilous situations. Taking a bottle from a determined drunk, she said later, was not unlike firmly taking a spear from an Indian. It was as well that she believed it because that is what she was frequently to find herself doing in the years to come.

All her friends and associates were startled by her announcement in 1948 that she was going to train to be a missionary in South America.

She had waited for seventeen years, the age she was when she had seen her brief vision on the deck of the *Aquitania*, and now forces beyond her power were stirring. This time her instructions were clear: the time was right and the place was right.

Rachel applied to study at the Oklahoma University Summer Institute of Linguistics course in the summer of 1948. The course was affiliated to the University, but not part of it. It had been the brain-child of Cameron Townsend, a man with an amazing capacity for a visionary outlook on life, and the faith to carry it through.

Cameron Townsend abandoned College to become a Bible salesman in Guatemala in 1917 at the age of twenty-one. Although his pay was $30 a month, he had to raise his own fare. After reaching Guatemala Townsend soon sold all his Bibles, and more.

There were greater things to come. He started up the first Protestant mission station, learned the language of the Cakchiquel Indians, the largest native group in Guatemala for whom there had never been, until then, a written language, and translated the New Testament into Cakchiquel.

By the time he was thirty-one he had opened schools, an orphanage, and an agricultural co-operative.

Having seen the way in which natives advanced rapidly in education once they had an alphabet and system of writing devised for their own language, Cameron Townsend decided that since there was no such discipline as the study of linguistics of *unknown* languages, he had better devise one. His enthusiasm, in the face of great obstacles, founded a summer training camp for the study of linguistics which developed into the Summer Institute of Linguistics (SIL). This, together with the Missionary Society which he also founded, became the Wycliffe Bible Translators (WBT), now the largest linguistic organization in the world, with over two thousand missionaries in the world's most isolated places, together with the huge back-up staff that supports them.

Cameron Townsend also had the vision to see that without an aviation support system, the work would be considerably slowed down. It can take a missionary and his wife three weeks to travel over rivers and rapids, while an aeroplane can cover the same distance in less than an hour. A vision with Cameron Townsend became a reality because he made it happen. He founded the Jungle Aviation and Radio Service (JAARS), the flying arms of SIL and WBT. He was still only forty years old.

It was to this dynamic and mushrooming organization that Rachel went to be a missionary.

For eleven weeks she studied sounds and syntax in an exhausting crash course. Some of the students with her in Oklahoma discussed where they hoped to go. In theory Rachel would go where she was sent, but she was not Katherine Proctor's daughter for nothing. There was just as much steely determination in Rachel Saint as there was in her mother, and if she felt that she was being sent to the wrong place, she would certainly protest.

She had long carried in her head like a motto the verse from Saint Paul's letter to the Romans: 'Those who have *never* been told of Him shall see and those who have *never* heard shall understand.'

From Oklahoma she packed her duffel bags and left for South Mexico and Boot Camp with the Lacondon Indians, the Wycliffe jungle training centre where all future missionary personnel are toughened up and carefully watched to ensure that they are the stuff of which missionaries must be made to survive the rigours of life in a hostile environment.

Rachel enjoyed the course. When she wrote to her older brother, Phil, who was already an evangelist in Argentina, that she was learning to drive a mule train, he replied that after fighting through her childhood with seven brothers, mules must be a cinch.

She was sent to Peru, where work with the Piro Indians, established by Cameron Townsend, was already in progress. She stopped off in Ecuador *en route* to visit her younger brother, Nate, who was a fully-fledged pilot working in conjunction with missionaries.

He had always been a very shy child, and his Botticelli features and candid gaze did not help; strangers were constantly stopping to admire him in the street. Visitors to the Saint house rarely saw him. He usually hid under his bed until they had gone.

It was probably his innate shyness that gave Nate such a love for the loneliness of the sky.

He was first taken up in an aeroplane shortly after his oldest brother, Sam, qualified as a pilot. Nate was so small that they gave him a box to perch on so that he could see the clouds from the cockpit. From that moment he became fanatical about flying, and since he was also an intensely religious boy, it was obvious that he was destined to be a jungle missionary pilot.

It was obvious, but not easy. There was the war. While Rachel wrestled with drunks, Nate wrestled with learning how to service planes in a huge hangar-factory. At the time he felt frustrated at not being old enough to fly, but later this mechanical training was interpreted by him as being God's preparation for the future when, alone in the jungle, he would have to be his own first-class mechanic. Finally, when he was able to take the Air Force pilot's entrance examination, he came sixth out of all the hundreds who had entered, but instead of being on his way to the USAF flying school in Texas, he found himself in hospital. An old bone infection had recurred and slivers of bone were working themselves out to the surface of his shin. The intense pain was no worse than his deep disappointment. For a while, he rejected his deep belief, and hated the world.

The culmination of his internal battle came when he had spent an entire night wandering about the streets of Detroit in a snow storm. In the morning, exhausted, he gave in. He sank to his knees in the snow and prayed, 'Lord, if it's your will that I never fly again, it's okay by me.'

Giving up all ideas of flying, Nate enrolled at Wheaton College for Bible Studies. It was there that he heard about the Missionary Aviation Fellowship, an organization still in its infancy, like Cameron Townsend's JAARS, which used small aeroplanes to open up inaccessible areas to missionaries. Nate needed no encouragement. He left Wheaton without completing his course, and enrolled at the Moody Bible Institute flight training school, and finally his dream came true when he joined the MAF.

Had he joined the United States Air Force, he would have been sent to the theatre of war and would have been dropping bombs. Instead, he was a pilot to missionaries.

Nate said that the bone infection that had put him in hospital had caused him great physical agony; if he had been responsible for dropping bombs on any human being, he would have suffered intense spiritual agony.

He was sent to Ecuador where work was in progress amongst the Oriente Indians of the south – the head-hunting Jivaros. His base was at Shell Mera, where he took his newly-acquired wife, Marj, and from whence, some years later, he was to fly to his death.

Not long after his arrival in Ecuador, a plane crash broke his back and made him blind. He said at the time: 'If I must be blind and crippled for the rest of my life in order that Indians may be saved, it is worth it all.'

This modest sacrifice was not to be; his sight gradually returned, and while still encased in plaster from neck to thigh, he returned to the jungle to build an advance mission base, and hack out an airstrip. The sun, blazing down on the airstrip once the protective trees had been cut down, made his cast so hot that he had to pour water into the plaster shell.

In Ecuador, Rachel was fascinated by Nate's work, and questioned him closely about his experiences. She felt a deep excitement beginning to stir when he told her of the almost completely unknown Aucas.

'I don't fly over them,' he said, 'I fly around them.'

A forced landing in any other part of the jungle would be dangerous, but not necessarily fatal, the greatest risk coming from the actual crash. A forced landing in Auca territory, he told Rachel, would mean almost certain death from their spears if he survived the landing.

'For a number of years the Aucas have constituted a hazard to explorers, an embarrassment to the Republic of Ecuador, and a challenge to missionaries of the Gospel,' wrote Nate in one of his reports.

Rachel wanted to know more, but Nate could add very little.

'They are an unknown people,' he said.

Rachel kept her excitement to herself. These were to be her people, she knew, but Wycliffe did not have a mission base in Ecuador then. When they did, she would be there, she told herself.

She continued south to Peru where she joined Esther Matteson who was working among the Piro Indians. From there, she went to work among the head-hunting Shapras whose chief, Tariri, was causing much concern to two young Wycliffe missionaries, Doris Cox and Loretta Anderson. The two girls had been with the Shapras for some years, and their translations were progressing well, but it was a personal tragedy for them that they had not been able to get through to the colourful Tariri. He allowed them to live and work with his tribe, but that did not stop him setting off with his feather-decked spears to do battle with his neighbours and take their heads as trophies.

Doris and Loretta needed a rest, but felt unable to leave their work. Rachel replaced one of them at a time and found that she got on quite well with Tariri.

There seemed to be a *rapport* between them, and during Rachel's two years' isolation with the Shapras, she had the satisfaction of seeing Tariri converted. He gave her a feather head-dress and later, when she met the President of Ecuador, Velasco Ibarra, to discuss working in Ecuador, she added a veil to the chief's gift and made a hat of it since she did not possess one, thinking that presidents deserved a certain amount of respect. Señor Ibarra was very entertained when Rachel spontaneously told him the story.

After Tariri's conversion, Rachel went on leave to stay with Nate in Ecuador. She had not seen him for two and a half years, and her first anxious questions were about the Aucas. Had anyone gone among them yet? she asked. 'No one,' Nate said. He went on to describe, instead, some recent attacks on Quichuas and Ecuadorian settlers living near the borders of their land in the jungle.

While travelling in Quito on buses, Rachel heard little else but discussions about the latest outbreak of Auca savagery. Nate introduced her to an oil engineer who told her that after several attacks on oil personnel surveying in the jungle, the company had withdrawn from their base at Arajuno. The engineer showed her a feather head-dress he had found after one such raid. It was exactly like the one chief Tariri had given her, and Rachel hoped that there might be some similarities in the two languages. It would be a help when she came to work with the Aucas.

That event, however, did not seem to be any closer as Wycliffe were still not in Ecuador.

Once back in Peru, Rachel went to Yarinacocha, the Wycliffe jungle base, to wait for new orders.

Over dinner she chatted to Catherine Peeke and Mary Sargent, who had been working on the Pastaza River near the Ecuadorian border; the Pastaza flows through Shell Mera on the Ecuadorian side where Nate was stationed.

Catherine asked Rachel where she would be going next, and Rachel hesitated for a moment.

'I'm not returning to the Shapras,' she said, audaciously. 'My tribe is across the border.'

'Across what border?'

'I'm going to work with the Aucas in Ecuador,' said Rachel in a quiet but firm voice.

Catherine and Mary were puzzled.

'But Wycliffe isn't working there.'

Later, towards the end of the meal, their director, Cameron Townsend, stood up to make an important announcement about a letter he had just received from the Ecuadorian ambassador to the United States, inviting them to work among the Indians of Ecuador.

After twenty-five years planning for such a moment, Rachel found when she arrived in Ecuador that she was apprehensive rather than elated. She had got so far, but now that she was actually in Quito, the Aucas seemed as far away as ever. She had to get into their territory without being foolhardy and risking lives. But how?

The answer seemed to come from Señor Carlos Sevilla whom Rachel had called on in his home in Quito to learn more about the Aucas.

Sevilla had had many close escapes from the Aucas, though not from their spears; his body was covered with deep scars, and his stories about his hair-raising adventures were legion. He was able to offer Rachel and Catherine Peeke more than just another story.

He called in one of his maids and Rachel was introduced to Joaquina, an Indian girl who had been captured by the Wagrani (as the Auca call themselves) and forced to live with them for fourteen months.

More than ten years had passed since Joaquina's escape from the Wagrani, and she had nearly forgotten the language. Sevilla saw that Rachel was disappointed. 'If you can make your way to the Hacienda Ila,' he told her, 'you can work with four real Auca girls who have fled from the jungle.'

Their names, he said, were Umi, Wiñaemi, Omiñia, and Dayuma.

Wagrani territory starts on the eastern slopes of the Andes.
RIGHT: Cloud vapour fills the narrow valleys.
OVERLEAF: Finding a Wagrani settlement by air is difficult. Few trees are cut down and 'villages' are small – this one was founded by Sam on the Cononaco

4

Dayuma's Childhood in the Jungle

THERE IS NO RECORDED TIME in the Amazon jungle. The years merge, one with another, unmeasured. There is no future, no past. Each life is like a pot of water scooped from the river. Wherever the pot is dipped, the water is the same. There are ripples and white rushes over rocks, dark depths and sandy shallows, but where the pot is dipped no one part of the water is different from another. The river is small at the beginning and big at the end; but who is to tell where is the end – who in the jungle has been to the end?

What memories there are go back to the natural seasons, not of spring and winter, for there is no spring, winter, or summer, but to the harvests of the fruit of the trees.

'The chonta palm has given its fruit five times since my father was speared, buried, and died,' or, 'When the kapok bursts and blows in the wind, then we will move our house'; these are the ways in which events are defined. Rarely more than five seasons past; never more than one season ahead, for who can say if he will live that long? No one knows how old they are when they die; and when they are alive they are the children, the adult, or the aged.

The young woman Akawo cared nothing for the past or the future as she spread her hammock close by the Fish River – the Tzapino – in the Season of the Fat Monkey. She bent and spread the large, clean banana leaves under the hammock, then straddled it, over the hole she had used before, cut in the tough fibre netting.

She had woven the hammock herself when a girl, married her husband, Caento, on it, and in time, when it was worn, had cut a hole and given birth

The simple huts are palm-walled and thatched – several families share, each
family having their own fire inside. These Wagrani have not had mission
contact, and practically none with outsiders

to her son. Now, she sat astride the hammock, her feet on the ground, leaning forward slightly, her hands gripping the sides and waited for the new baby to drop to the leaves.

She was alone, her hammock tied to two trees in a small clearing not far from the palm-leaf houses. She didn't know her own age and would soon forget the age of Wawae, the boy child who was her first-born. She knew nothing of the world beyond her own world, the centre of all life, the land of the Wagrani. The distant mountains of evening and the morning sky marked the edge of the world.

There was nothing to tell her as she waited in the rich damp, in the quietly buzzing heat, that thousands of miles away in cold northern waters, to the east beyond the rising sun, another young woman as fair as she was dark, had felt the pull of a cord that was to bind her to the coming child.

The child came, and she cut the cord with a sharp clam shell, then examined it critically. It was another girl child, but she would keep it, for the older girl no longer needed all her milk. It seemed healthy, too. If it were deformed or weak, she would have scooped a hole in the soft loam of the clearing and casually buried it. Covered with earth, it would soon die. Some women strangled their unwanted babies with vines and then threw them into the bushes, or simply left them on the trail. After burying the child, Akawo could bathe in the river, fold her hammock and return to the huts; none would comment and the baby would soon be forgotten.

But the tiny girl was healthy. She tied the bark-cloth sling that she had ready round her, then slipped the baby in, giving it a breast to suck. She left the placenta where it had dropped; it would soon be eaten by insects. Then she stepped in the shallows of the river and washed herself and the baby, scooping handfuls of water over its sticky head until it was clean.

'What will you call the child?' Caento, her husband, asked when he returned from his hunt.

'Dayuma. I shall call her Dayuma after my grandmother who was killed,' Akawo said.

It was the custom to call children after relatives and Grandmother Dayuma had been shot by outsiders when Akawo's father, Caento, was still a small child. Grandfather Karae, his wife, Dayuma, and their two young children were in a family hunting party with other relatives when some cannibal outsiders, armed with guns, had opened fire on them. Grandfather Karae, who was then a young man, saw his daughter die at once, and as her mother, Karae's wife, bent to pick her up, she also was shot and killed. Grandfather Karae was shot deep across his stomach, an ugly wound that split his viscera open and exposed his liver.

He felt no immediate pain, so snatched up his small son, Caento, who was to become Akawo's father, and fled across river with him, his blood bathing them both and attracting the flies that laid eggs in his open gut. Before he got better he was alive with maggots and thought he would die. He begged to be buried so that his body would not rot above ground, but his people, who killed as casually as they ate, decided he would recover with care and with care they watched over him. He was spared, and lived.

Akawo's father and husband both shared the name Caento, after a common relative. Akawo and her husband were first cousins, children of sisters as was the custom.

Now she was calling her new daughter Dayuma; a girl who was to grow up to help focus the whole world's attention on one of the remotest and most dangerous people in the world, a tribe who were unknown because few dared penetrate their borders.

Dayuma spent the first two years of her life close-pressed against her mother's body in the bark-cloth sling. A milky breast was always available, and her mother's body was warm and comforting, especially in the early hours when the chill river mist crept round their open hut.

The bark-sling was both carry-cot and napkin and as a small baby her loose stools soaked through and ran down Akawo's hip and thigh. They were never far from water, and it was little problem for Akawo to step into water, herself and infant, and wash. It was no problem, either, to replace the cloth: merely to peel another strip of the sacking-like material from under the bark of the tree.

As the child grew older, she was held away from her mother's body for toilet training and washed immediately after in a small gourd, her mother cupping her hands and scooping the water over the child as she squatted on her haunches. If the child stooled in the house, on the earth floor, the mess was kicked to one side, where all the bones and feathers and other food waste was thrown, to be eaten by ants and termites in a few hours. The adults voided themselves in the river; it was quick and hygienic.

Water played a large part in Dayuma's life. Her people washed themselves constantly and when her mother wasn't working she was playing in the water with her children. When she swam, she pushed the baby, still in her sling, on to her back, and so from her earliest moments the child knew the rivers of her home.

Washing wasn't only to keep clean, or to play; they were plagued by flying insects that bit and stung, and in the water there was a certain freedom from the constant irritation.

As the months passed Dayuma learned to leave the close comfort of her mother's body, but there was always another body, another thigh to sit on and cling to. No child was put down and left. Little children carried those smaller than themselves in a sling, or clutched them in the wide family hammocks. Aunts, grandmothers, fathers, all took and held a small child so that crying was for a good reason and not for the sake of outrage or anger.

Children who cried came to a very rapid end, although they weren't aware of the end results of their misery. They were choked with vines in the jungle to silence them and then thrown into the bushes. 'What good is a child who cries? It must be sick', was the casual reasoning, and when asked where a missing child was the answer would be, 'The baby died alone in the jungle.'

Natani, one of Dayuma's aunts, was bored with her crying child and she left it on a riverside hill. Nobody commented on the fact for some weeks, then her father asked where the child was, but Natani simply shrugged. Later when she had another baby, her father said, 'Watch out, don't you throw this one away,' so the child lived to grow up.

Moipa was a notorious killer and one of his wives, Aka, showed very little interest in her children. She threatened to tie two, a boy and a girl, together by their hands and feet and leave them where outsiders would find and take them. A crying child was later buried alive by her.

Moipa had been on a killing raid and when he returned he asked where the baby was, but Aka shrugged.

'The baby cried and cried when we went to the jungle. We dug in the ground and buried her,' Aka's mother said.

Moipa was angry. He had just come from a killing raid, but saw no reason for his child to die.

'Later she will bear another child,' Aka's mother said, comfortably. 'She threw this one away for no good reason. Later she will have another.'

By the time Dayuma's younger brother was born, she had learnt to walk, clinging to her mother's leg and following her wherever she went.

She had no toys, nor did any of the children, girls or boys.

Play was active and was usually in the water. Her mother had taught her to swim by taking her out of the sling and laying her across her back until they were in deep water, then she loosed the little girl's arms and supported her lightly. Dayuma was so used to water that she had no reason to be afraid, and so, she swam. She was soon like a fish, and would look for small fish and crayfish in the shallows, while the older children dived under water for bigger fish which were caught by hand, with a lot of laughter.

The family would go on hunting parties, deep into the jungle, walking in single file along the well-worn jungle trails. All the time her eyes were sharpening, and she and her small brothers and sisters saw movements where none seemed to be. Dayuma would not ever have to hunt herself, with blowpipe and poison-tipped dart; like her mother, she would go for company and to help carry. But for her brothers, it was a more serious affair. They would have to keep their families in meat and half their lives would be given to hunting.

Caento made the boys small, but very heavy, blowpipes from the solid chonta palm. Their weight was remarkable, but the children balanced them with ease. They had small dart cases with closely-fitting lids to keep the poison curare dry and carefully mimicked their father. By the time the boys were into their eighth kapok season they were expert and excellent hunters, able to go out on their own and return with a kill.

Their play, when they weren't hunting, involved taking small pieces of wood and aiming them at some small, trapped creature, like a frog or a long-eared mouse, until it was riddled with tiny holes. Dayuma would watch her mother weave hammocks and net baskets – *chigras*. She watched her make the string from Chambira palm leaves, rolling the strands, split like raffia, over her knees to twist the thread, and rolling these strands with other strands to make thicker or thinner fibre as was required. She watched her gather the wild cotton and spin it by hand in the afternoons while lolling on her hammock. The material was never used for clothes, but for lighter baskets or for decorative bands. She would watch her mother cut the yucca stalks into portions, each bearing a bud, with her sharp stone knife and then plant this in a hole made in the ground simply with the point of another stick.

The men cleared the ground, cutting down huge forest giants with their primitive stone axes or stolen axes of steel when they could get hold of them.

The stone axes made for slow work; sometimes a really big tree took several months to hack to the ground. The stone axes seemed to chew and gnaw the fibres of the trunk, rather than cut cleanly into it. A steel axe would do the same job in under an hour, and it wasn't surprising that steel was jealously guarded and yearned for. Where the trees fell, they were left, their branches being hacked off and piled up with the undergrowth and burnt. In time the trees rotted, or, with a big work party, they were rolled to one side, and so a clearing of a sort was made. It was a clearing with uneven earth, roots, tree trunks, but rarely rocks. In the spaces, yucca was planted, as well as sweet potato, ground nut and sweet wild banana and plantain, although, more frequently, the latter two were found in natural 'plantations' in the jungle and not specifically cultivated. The women and their children tentatively weeded their crops, though by the time the yucca shrubs had grown above their heads, the shade from the spreading branches, kept the ground relatively free of weeds.

There was no real reason why the men and boy children should hunt and build and the women and girl children till the land and make the hammocks. There was no cultural law about it, but it worked out like that. Small boys trapped little animals and tormented them with sharp sticks; small girls nursed the babies of the tribe and played with strips of palm leaf and learned to weave. None was forced; each could do as they wanted, and girls copied their mothers and boys their fathers, new generation after new generation, each in their turn.

Punishment was infrequent but firm. It didn't involve a raised voice or outburst of rage. Children who behaved badly were whipped all over with stinging nettles, or they had burning red pepper wiped in their eyes. The stinging nettles, like most plants of the Amazon, were bigger than their temperate counterparts; their stings were anything up to an inch long and proportionately more painful.

Dayuma's cousin, Umi, was her usual companion and the two little girls often did things they were told not to do. One of their favourite games was to slide down the nearly vertical red clay slope of a landslide that headed straight into deep river water. The slope was so steep that they had to haul themselves up with vines, and after a rain it was treacherous, with sharp, up-pointing snapped-off roots and stumps, the earth constantly threatening to slide again. One day, while the children were playing on the slope, there was another slip, and tons of earth narrowly missed them.

The children were delighted with the danger, but their adult relatives were not so entertained. The children had been warned often enough, and their Uncle Kiwa went to look for them, following the sound of their delight. He applied nettles all over their body until they thought they would never recover, and they promised they would never behave so foolishly again.

No sooner had the pain died down than the children decided to punish Kiwa in revenge. He had gone out hunting, and they knew the path by which he would return. Weary, laden with his heavy blowgun and monkeys slung about his shoulders, Kiwa returned in the evening to step on wicked thorns planted by the children on the path. The thorn of the chonta palm is up to three inches long; they pierced even his thick soles.

He nettled the children until they were a mass of red weals, and no sooner were these better than revenge was required. They went to his peanut patch and ate a large quantity. The theft was discovered, and more nettles were cut.

In this family way of punishment and revenge, unknowingly the children were emulating the more dangerous activity of their elders, where a death led to a killing, and a killing led to retaliation. The honour of sisters, brothers, uncles, aunts, cousins and third cousins were settled by a spear attack. The victim was killed and then *his* honour had to be appeased. Not only were enemies destroyed in this orgy of spearing, but, if a son was killed, then his father would spear a 'useless' daughter, sister or grandmother to compensate for his grief. Then he would go and revenge himself upon his enemies.

If a father were killed, his son, however young and however many years had passed, would, sooner or later, seek out his enemy and woo him with sweet words, then kill him with pleasure.

Although Kiwa was a relative, Dayuma was quite delighted when he was speared by the dangerous Moipa. He had recently married, and had a baby daughter, but Dayuma's pleased reaction to his death was to ask, 'Now, who will nettle us?'

There was no shortage of applicants. Her other uncle, Gikita, proved every bit as energetic as Kiwa, grabbing the little girls by their long hair. Finally Dayuma took a sharp clam shell and hacked her hair short so that Gikita had nothing to grab. The other girls followed suit, and, for a while, all the daughters of the tribe had cropped locks.

The game went against them. With their ears exposed, the adults decided it was time that they were pierced, ready for the balsa plugs that would fit in place as they got older and the lobes stretched.

There was no correct time, as at birth or puberty, for the piercing to take place. In fact, a common time was when children were being troublesome, or when someone remembered – and they usually only remembered *when* children were being unusually naughty.

'Okay, time for a good piercing session,' was approximately how the conversation went: 'Round up the kids; perhaps a hole in the ear will make them act like adults.'

A long, sharp chonta thorn was used – the same thorn that the children had planted on the trail for their dead uncle, Kiwa. The thorn was pressed hard through the lobe to its widest part and moved around to enlarge the hole. It hurt, and the children yelled. There was no cult of the stoic amongst them. Like the children they were, if a thing was amusing, they laughed, and if it hurt, they cried. When the hole was made, a rolled leaf, the juices of which stung the wound, was inserted, and over the years this was gradually enlarged until the hole took a balsa plug up to three inches in diameter. Sometimes the wound was infected by small worms, and these helped enlarge it, although care had to be taken that the lobe was not eaten away entirely.

The balsa plugs were normally painted with white lime found in the river, and were worn at all times. In this respect, unlike any of their neighbours, the Wagrani were like the Inca, the Peruvian royal house, where only members of the ruling class had pierced ears. In their case, the hole was large enough to insert a solid gold disc.

All members of the tribe wore the plugs, men and women, older boys and girls. The Wagrani had no chief, no leader. Sometimes a member of a group was stronger than the others and became a leader in a way, but that was because he killed more energetically and so was more dangerous and feared. It seemed that some men, like Moipa, and like Wepe whom Dayuma had heard of but never seen since he lived in a different part of the jungle, had a blood-lust in their bones. Wepe, certainly, if the stories she had heard were accurate, was affected by the full moon at which time he would kill for pleasure, travelling at speed, even to the borders of the land, looking for outsiders.

There were many games that Dayuma's father, Caento, taught them. They swam in the Fish River, ignoring the dangers of the dark-snouted caymans; they were slow and fun to poke, so they hit them with sticks, and poked them with poles as they lay, fat and sleepy on the sandbanks. And the caymans would swim lazily away and sink to the clay at the bottom of the river. Even the notorious piranha were not dangerous in those rivers and were easily caught, or vanished into the depths.

The one thing they all feared was the water boa, the anaconda, who had no fear of anything that lived. His coils terrified the Wagrani, and when one was seen, they scattered, leaving a victim, if already trapped, to his fate.

In later years Dayuma's younger brother, Nampa, was crushed by a boa while out hunting. He finally managed to escape from its coils, but was so badly crushed that his whole body was black with bruising and haemorrhage. He lingered in great pain for a month before dying.

Another game taught by Caento was deep pool diving, when the children grasped heavy stones and sank to the bottom of the deepest part of the river under the sandstone cliffs. Those who stayed down the longest did best, although the Wagrani didn't have a competitive spirit. They did difficult things for the pleasure of doing them and they enjoyed danger if it was fun and not for the sake of being 'better' than anyone else. They never got angry with anyone who succeeded where they had failed.

The diving practice was more than just a game, too. It helped them catch

All the children enjoy looking after the babies. Obi is about 14. Of her, Sam says 'she's always there to help, loves to fool around, is a great sport and is as lively as a humming-bird'

Fire is valued in the jungle and a termites' nest is particularly useful for its smouldering properties – constructed of dried leaves in a honeycomb design. Small pieces are broken off and carried many miles in a pot, ready to start a fire where needed. When flying insects become too annoying, children run around with burning fragments to make protective smoke-screens.

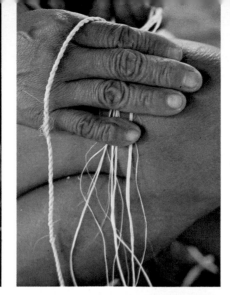
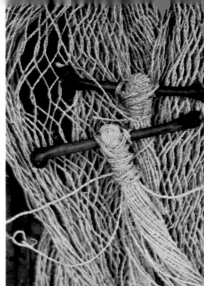

String, mainly used for hammocks and carrying baskets *(chigra)* is made from the split leaf of the chambira palm. It is hung up to dry like rafia, then rolled over the knee – generally an afternoon occupation of women, while stories are told. Hammocks are suspended from smoked monkey bones and woven by women between two upright sticks. Anything up to eight feet wide, both parents and one or two children sleep diagonally together for warmth. Nights are chilly and no covers are used. This woman shares her husband with another. Although young, she has her ears pierced – a custom which is dying out

fish underwater. It was rare to go underwater fishing with a spear, although spears were sometimes used in the shallows. Quite big fishes were caught by hand. Simple rods were used as well. Thin palm-leaf twine, like the type used to hang monkey teeth around their necks, was tied to the end of a long pole cut from the bushes on the bank. A piece of sharpened and shaped shell was attached to the twine and fat white grubs from rotten palm trunks used initially for bait until a small fish was caught. It was simple but effective.

Nets were sometimes woven by Wagrani who had watched the Quichua, Indians from the outside, fish. The nets were flat, woven like a *chigra*, and fastened to a bent wood frame that looked like a lacrosse stick.

The method that yielded the greatest catch was to dam up a small stream and then to pour the stunning poison, barbasco, into the water upstream. The fish were drugged, or stunned, and floated to the surface, where they were scooped up, either by hand, or with nets, at the dam. Barbasco was a small shrub and the green leaves, rather like that of the mulberry, were pounded with a stick on the ground until they looked like regurgitated cud. This was collected in a gourd and tipped in the water. Fish that weren't wanted for food were left and eventually recovered, unless first eaten by other predators.

Dayuma's initial good health wasn't to last; debilitating fevers came to the tribe and left her weak and thin. While others died, or recovered, she remained sickly, lingering long hours on her hammock. This irritated her mother who had a growing family to care for and who never knew when her husband might be killed by his enemy, Moipa, who had moved to an upriver area. She couldn't afford to have a sickly child.

Even if Caento were not killed, the Wagrani needed to be fit to survive their nomadic way of life. They travelled from one harvest to another, from one yucca patch to another. As one area was depleted of its game, they moved on, eventually returning to all their houses in turn.

The land they travelled, much of it not far from the foothills of the great snow-covered mountain peaks, which could be seen from the river, was very rough terrain. There were steep hills and deep gorges that made already difficult jungle travel more difficult. It was not good to have an ailing child who needed constant rest, and who couldn't keep up with a fast-moving party. If Dayuma had not already grown past the age for an easy death, Akawo knew she could find it very easy to kill her.

Dayuma was her father's favourite child, and with him she was secure.

TOP LEFT: The last Zapáro, now living with Wagrani. When she dies, her tribe will be extinct. TOP RIGHT: An elderly relation of Dayuma and Sam who is also a close friend of Akawo, Dayuma's mother. Balsa plugs are rarely used in the ears today. BOTTOM LEFT: Beards are uncommon – they are plucked out. Hair is cut with a clam shell. BOTTOM RIGHT: Achiote seed pods make a red stain, used for decoration and an insect repellent. Unlike most Wagrani, this girl's teeth are in good shape.

When she was well he took her hunting with her brothers and they slowed their normal pounding trot to suit her breathless lungs. She curled up close to him in the hammock when the fevers made her shake with cold, and he understood. At night he fed the fire, burning close by the hammocks, to keep the river chill away.

They had no covers, no clothes, and depended in the cold dawn hours on the warmth of three or more fires, one for each group sharing their long houses.

Caento had been missing for seven days and Dayuma was worried. She was worried about her father, certain that he was dead, and she was worried about her own life.

Her father had gone hunting upriver where he thought he would get a good kill of wild white-lipped peccary, a small jungle pig. It was true that a hunter was often away for many days, especially when he was on the trail of good game, but it was unusual for a man to be away so long when travelling alone. For one thing, he would have too many days to travel, carrying heavy meat, which would surely putrefy long before he returned home. Perhaps he was hurt, Dayuma thought hopefully, and was moving slowly.

She looked anxiously at her mother Akawo, trying to assess her mood.

Akawo had a surly expression. The smoked monkey tail* had long been devoured, and her oldest son, Wawae, had killed only one guan, the black and white wild turkey, which was small and had little enough meat. The boy was sick with another fever that was sweeping the group and couldn't hunt. She herself had caught fish, but fish didn't satisfy her hungry children and her old mother, Ipanai, and the even older father of her husband, Grandfather Karae, as did the solid, meaty muscles of a big monkey or a tree sloth.

Wawae's skin was yellow and he shivered constantly. Perhaps he would die. Perhaps some of the children and the old people would die. Then, if Caento, her husband, failed to return, she, Akawo, would live by catching fish and eating yucca until she married again.

Many of her cousins were already married, but there was no problem in that; she would become their second, or third wife. It was good to share the work with another woman.

There were too many children; perhaps the fever would not kill them. Dayuma was thin and weak, and for many moons had not been much help to her. If the children did not die, she would kill Dayuma first.

'If your father doesn't return by tomorrow, I will kill you,' she told the

* Smoked monkey tail is reputed to cure bad hearts.

girl. 'I will strangle you with a vine and stuff your body in a rotten tree trunk.'

Dayuma spent the night curled up in the hammock with her younger sisters, Nimu and Gimari. Would her mother kill them also, if Caento failed to return? They were plump and strong, but they were young and could do little work. All they could do was eat and swim. Dayuma knew that if Moipa had speared her father and left him, unburied, in the jungle, even now he could be on his way downriver to kill them all as was the custom. Women and their children had no special consideration; they were part of the man, and if he was killed, in time they too, were killed.

The movements of the night-hunting animals, the splashes of the caymans in the river, the big turtles swimming; each sound was a threat.

Dawn was a long, slow light, mist-filled and quiet. The shifting children huddled closer together and complained of the cold until Akawo fanned up the fire with the black turkey-tail fan and put on the big clay pot of water ready for the first meal of the day. She was worried, and in a childish way was taking her fear out on Dayuma, her father's favourite child.

'Today, if he does not come, I will kill you,' she said. 'If your father doesn't come, then surely Moipa will come, and I cannot travel with a broken reed.'

Then the other children were frightened and their voices sharpened into whines as they all talked at once about Moipa and how they would escape him.

Dayuma decided there was very little difference between being speared by Moipa or strangled by her mother; she would run away and live with the wild deer. She could not hunt, but she could catch fish and freshwater prawns. There were bananas and papaya all the time, and other fruits in their season. If she travelled, she would find patches of yucca and sweet potato, and could eat them as well. She could make fire with a fire stick, and her mother had long ago taught her how to weave her own hammock. She could make a small hut to shelter her from the wild jungle storms. She would take her small spider-monkey for a companion, and a macaw to warn her of danger, and in that way she would live. Free from the threats of her mother and the hatred of their enemies.

It was a good plan. No child had ever run away before, but Dayuma, although she was not aware of it, was not a usual Wagrani child. From birth, she had been destined to be different from the others, and there was a pattern to her life that had been set in motion even before her birth.

Caento returned before noon.

There had been no game, although he had followed many tracks, and without meat he could not return to his family. He had travelled long and far, sleeping on the ground at night, even in the path of the ants. He had soon eaten his yucca paste, and for two days he had been hungry. Then he had seen the great howler monkey, a group of them, and had killed four before the rest fled through the high branches. He had smoked the meat, but it was two days old. Now the family must eat it quickly.

In that way, he told them the story of his hunt as he drank the sweet banana drink, thick and sticky in the gourd. Then he repeated the story with gestures, his face alight as he pointed high with his arm, to the trees where the monkeys had been. The story was told again, all morning. It was a thing to talk of, as were all hunting stories. They made up the rhythm of the life in the jungle. Anything, however small, was discussed time and time again until something else came to take its place.

When she had a moment, Dayuma told her father about her mother's threat: 'Now I am back,' Caento said. 'Now it is all right.'

He was not angry with Akawo. She must do what she must; that was the way of the Wagrani.

'We thought Moipa had speared you,' Dayuma said. 'We thought he would come and spear us.'

Caento's face darkened. 'Moipa is upriver now,' he said. 'And I was upriver also, but I did not see him. Moipa is bad, I have told him that, many times. Our people kill too much, it's not good. Moipa marries many wives, and those he does not want, he kills. It is good to kill an enemy, but soon there will be no young women left for our young men to marry. No, Moipa is not good.'

Dayuma looked at her father's outburst nervously. She knew that Moipa was her father's bitterest enemy. Her father was not a killer. Moipa was, and he was cunning.

5

Inter-tribal Warfare and Dayuma's Escape to the Outside

THERE WERE SEVERAL HUNDRED WAGRANI at that time living between Curaray and Tiwaeno; the huts were larger then, and there were ten of them. In one hut lived Dayuma's family with ten other families; men with their wives and children.

It was a short period of peace. Babies were being born, and the tribe increasing.

The small boy Aentyaeri was a member of Dayuma's family group. His father was a witch doctor. Witch doctors lived a precarious life amongst the Wagrani. On the one hand they were important and their word was listened to, and on the other they were held responsible for introducing the devils that caused death. Before a man died of sickness, his heirs, his sons, would come close to him and ask, 'Who is the witch doctor who has done this?' and the imagined name would be whispered. Later, if the opportunity occurred, the witch doctor would be speared.

So it was with Aentyaeri's father. Mingi speared him in revenge for an imagined bit of bad magic. Aentyaeri and his little brother watched from their hiding place as first their father, and then their mother, were killed in the forest where they had been ambushed. When it was safe, the two small boys shivered near the bodies of their parents, then returned to their empty, fireless hut and huddled together. Not understanding what death was, they returned time and again to their parents, until the bodies decayed and vultures descended to tear at the putrid meat.

Caento's father eventually took in the hungry orphans and raised them with his family in the years before Dayuma was born.

Aentyaeri grew in height and strength. His reputation as a hunter grew. He married and moved from the Fish River but all the time the desire was in him to kill Mingi who had moved far into the forest, and was out of reach of his spears.

When Mingi returned to the Curaray and heard that the small boy Aentyaeri was now a warrior, he decided to kill him first before he himself was killed.

When Aentyaeri heard of Mingi's return, he went to the old witch doctor, Karae, Dayuma's grandfather, and asked his advice.

The witch doctor told him, 'Kill him if you want; if you don't want to kill him, don't.'

'I'll kill him,' Aentyaeri said.

He was remembering a recent visit to his foster-mother, the woman who had brought up the two small orphans. He had found her rotting body stuffed into a hollow tree, the victim of a spearing. He had no reason to blame Mingi for her death, but his anger was hot within him.

Aentyaeri planned a raid, and took his brother and Moipa with him. Mingi, also, was planning a raid, and had his supporters with him. Aentyaeri struck first and killed the man who had killed his parents. His revenge was beginning. He travelled through the jungle looking for all Mingi's former companions in the old days when his parents had been killed. The toll of victims rose. By the next morning in Caento's clearing alone there were the bodies of twenty-two dead or dying Wagrani, including small children.

Caento dug a large hole and buried them all.

The ground was now prepared for a long period of revenge; everyone who had a dead relative had to kill in retaliation. By the end of the period, four huts remained and less than a hundred people.

Dayuma was a small child when she saw her first killing. It was a grey early morning. The jungle grass was wet with rain that had fallen in the night, and the children had woken early, unable to sleep through the cold that struck into their bellies. Dayuma crept out of her hammock, careful not to disturb the sleeping groups, and ran to the house of her friend, Gomoki. The little children gathered in a group in one corner of the house, playing quietly together with sticks and stones. Moipa shared that hut. He was now an experienced killer. Dayuma looked up to see him and an accomplice close in silently on the hammock in which Gomoki's father slept. In her childish way she knew something was wrong. She saw them blink their eyes as a signal and then they struck in unison. The blood spread through the strands of the hammock, dripping on the mud floor. First the blood of Gomoki's father, then her mother, and then her baby sister, all speared while they were still heavy in sleep. The children playing in the corner fled through the hanging walls of the hut, and hid in the vines of the forest.

They returned later, when the sun was high and the flies buzzing. Akawo and Caento were there. Gomoki's father was not dead. The spears had entered his body and throat so that he could not speak.

'Shall we bury him now?' Akawo asked.

'He may live,' Caento said. But he did not. It took him many days to die.

Caento took three orphans to live with him from that killing. Now he had four adopted children to feed, including Aepi, a captured Quichuan girl; a heavy burden for a man to carry who had to hunt for meat single-handed.

Moipa was angry that some of the family had survived. He wanted to kill them all so that none could grow up to kill him. He waited until the children were playing alone, then he speared the three-year-old sister of Gomoki, pinning her to the ground. He could not withdraw his spear, so he grabbed Gomoki and Aepi and played a cruel game with them, attempting to kill them in a slow, torturing way. He bound them together with vines, and threw them in the river. Just as they were on the point of drowning, he fished them out, waited until they had recovered a little, and threw them back in. Dayuma was watching from the shadows of the bushes on the river bank, and ran to fetch her father.

Caento confronted Moipa, and weaponless, the killer broke away and plunged into the jungle. The two girls appeared to be dead when Caento pulled them out of the water, their bellies huge and distended. Dayuma pushed with all her weight, and the water gushed out. When they recovered, Caento ordered them never to leave his side. When he hunted, they were to hunt; when he swam, they were to swim. From that day the two little girls followed him about the jungle like faithful hounds.

Moipa made an uneasy peace with his neighbours. He avoided Caento, but with low cunning he made friends with the adolescent Wawae, Dayuma's favourite brother. It was Moipa's way to make friends with any young blood he thought would be useful to him later, and he also developed a friendship with Itaeki, who had been Aentyaeri's disciple. Aentyaeri had been killed by outsiders shortly after he had initiated the inter-tribal battle in which Mingi was killed.

Whilst hunting, Moipa saw a red and white aeroplane flying over the Curaray where the river plunged down from the hills. He followed it with his eyes from his position nearly a hundred feet up a tree where he had swarmed with his blowgun to shoot monkey, and he saw bundles falling from the plane. Curious, abandoning his monkey in a cooling stream until his return, he ran swiftly to where he had seen the bundles fall. They led him to a Negro, a lone man, chopping trees. He watched for a while, then faded into the undergrowth. He did not know it, but the Negro, a Shell Oil employee, was preparing the land for a geological team to drill. The bundles contained supplies for him.

Moipa collected a small group of men about him, their differences forgotten for a while. They did not want any foreigner in their land cutting their trees and shooting their game.

When they returned in the evening, the black foreigner was sitting quietly by his fire strumming a guitar. They killed him quickly and stole his clothes. Moipa and Wawae put on the strange garments at once, proud of their prize. They wore the clothes night and day, never removing them until they rotted on their bodies and dropped off. They had no idea that clothes should be washed.

Caento was not happy with the raids on which his son, Wawae, was going. He had a dislike of killing, of causing attention to be paid to them, and he thought that sooner or later the foreigners would send in a large retaliatory hunting party. He remembered a raid he had gone on with Moipa before he grew to dislike him. A large group of them, including Wawae, had left the Curaray, and gone to the Arajuno River where there was a Shell Oil camp.

Moipa had already been there and had speared six workers. Then they returned to finish them off, and to see what they could steal. They needed axes and machetes; there were not enough to go round.

The camp was deserted when they arrived, the men having been withdrawn after Moipa's attack. The Wagrani plundered the houses, destroying all they did not want. They tasted the contents of sacks of flour and rice, and discarded them. They dipped their fingers in the sugar and promptly threw it away. They left with tools and blankets and cooking pots. The blankets were soon rejected because they 'stank'.

Caento was worried about the increasing activity on the borders of their land, convinced that their raids on the outside were causing it, and he did not understand what the aeroplanes were. The tribe spent hours at night discussing what they could be. They knew the objects were alive, or they could not fly like bees or birds through the sky. They called them 'wood-bees' because they buzzed, but they knew they were not bees. Bees did not have people inside their bodies.

Most of them decided, finally, that they were like the vampire devil bats of their legends, and that they carried devil cubs within them. In their legends, devils took strange shapes, animal or human, and in their legends the devils were cannibals, like the outsiders. There was not much to choose between them, although they thought they knew where they were with an outsider, while a devil from an aeroplane who had assumed human shape was to be watched with caution.

Caento was worried by many things, but most of all he was worried about Moipa. He knew that he would attempt to kill him one day, and so every day he had to walk with care and with fear at his shoulder. No longer could he relax in his hammock at night, or swim in the river, at ease with his children.

When his hunting brought him no meat, he was convinced that Moipa had been to a witch doctor who had put a curse upon him. He shot a poison-tipped dart into a monkey, and it did not die, although the curare was well-made and potent. The curse was a strong one.

Caento told his daughter that soon Moipa would kill him. 'What shall I do then?' Dayuma asked. 'Shall I stay here, or shall I leave the Land?'

'Go away from here,' Caento said. 'Go to foreigners. You are a child. They will take care of you. It is better that way.' Unusual words for a Wagrani.

The storm approached in a straight line across the tree-tops. Dayuma saw the clouds marching towards her as if the distant mountains were moving, closing in on the small settlement. The air boiled and churned, and the solid clouds soared higher against the plum-coloured sky. As the clouds climbed up, the water from the sky fell down, blotting out the trees. In a moment Dayuma was surrounded by water as if it were raining from the earth and sky. Her mother, Akawo, lay on her hammock in the hut, moaning, her leg swollen with the poison from a sting-ray. The little ones, Nampa and Bimari, were playing on the mud floor, plaiting wands, but Dayuma's sister, Onaenga, was fishing in the river close by, while further downstream were her father, Caento, and her brother, Wawae.

Onaenga fled from the river ahead of the great winds and sheets of lightning. The blast nearly flattened her as she reached the family hut, and the palm thatch was lifted and whirled away.

Dayuma saw that if the trees fell across the clearing, there would be nothing to stop them crashing on the hut, so she grabbed Nampa and called to Onaenga to take Bimari, and the two girls ran towards the trees.

The savage wind beat down the tall trees before it. Dayuma passed into the protection of the forest, but a tree fell on Onaenga and she was killed. Akawo, hobbling behind, escaped by hurling herself into a bramble patch, where she sobbed in terror.

The storm from the mountains passed, but another storm was brewing on the Curaray.

Caento and old Karae, Dayuma's sister Gimari, and others in the family went on an overnight journey to their yucca patch. They arrived at dusk and had a simple meal of smoked monkey tail and maize roasted on a fire which they had carried with them in their *chigras*.

Gimari had carried the fire pot, a small bowl of smouldering termite nest which glowed for hours and quickly fanned into a blaze when needed. They planned to be away for several days, for they had to weed the *chacra*, plant new yucca, and prepare the bundles of harvested roots to carry home.

They had no hammocks with them, but curled up in the shelters formed by the giant fanning buttress roots of the pepper kapok tree (*uchu putu*). The tree itself was relatively slender, soaring up in smooth grey-barked splendour to dizzy heights where the yellow orioles hung their long nests, but the roots formed a high-walled star pattern, whose sides were as tall as a room, and narrow, like a fence. They were frequently eighteen feet in extent, radiating from the central trunk.

After the meal, the group settled down for the night. They had travelled a long way and were weary, and in the morning there would be much work. What none of them realized was that Moipa had trailed them every inch of the way.

It was dark and shadowy in the shelters of the tree roots. Moipa wanted to kill Caento first, for he was powerful in body. Then he wanted to kill the old grandfather Karae next, for his spirits were strong. But it was dark and he could not see well. Also, the party had foolishly scattered themselves in separate compartments, and he could not get them simultaneously.

Old Karae was killed at once, and Caento was speared in his knees. The others fled into the jungle, not knowing that Moipa was alone. Moipa did not stay to see what damage he had done. He knew that he had hit Caento; now he wanted to kill the others before they could prepare themselves to resist.

He turned and raced along the trail. It was a day's march back to the settlement, and they were all weary, but the hunted fled through the night with the hunter behind them. Dayuma heard them calling in the morning as she awoke from sleep. She knew at once that something was wrong although she could not make out any words, and she ran out of the gloom of the hut into the grey half-light outside and hid. Akawo took her baby, Oba, and with another son, Nampa, ducked through the rear exit of the hut. An old uncle was left, and some of the little ones who did not understand what was happening. Those who had run through the night to warn the others fanned out as they reached the hut, and took to the forest, leaving a clear path for Moipa who rushed yelling into the hut, hacking about with his machete. He killed the old uncle with one thrust, then hacked all the children to bloody pieces. Akawo had left her youngest daughter, Nimu, in her hammock, and the little girl was slashed into portions as if she were a monkey prepared for the pot. When it was safe to return, Akawo burnt the house down, rather than bury the dead.

Dayuma heard the cries from the hut; she did not know what was happening, and did not know that her father had been wounded, and her grandfather killed. She remembered what her father had said, how they had agreed that when Moipa came, she would leave. She wasted no time now. With the small group who had left the hut with her, she made her way to the beach on the Curaray where some canoes, stolen in the past from river travellers, were moored. The mist lay thick over the water, and heron moved off in lazy flight, disturbed by their agitated rustles as they hastily hacked at bamboo to make poles. The river was high, and the current caught them as they swept into mid-stream. They needed the poles only to guide them, and to push the canoe away from great half-submerged trees and sandbanks.

They had no food, no possessions; a group of naked children in the middle of a river before the sun was up, rushing they knew not where. It was frightening, and they were scared.

The rivers in the Amazon jungle do not flow in straight lines; they double back upon themselves in astonishing convolutions. Two points, twenty miles apart by river, can be less than half a mile apart across country. The benefit of travelling by river was that it was safer, and in this case, Dayuma needed the canoe to make her way to freedom.

She had been travelling for a day when ahead of her she saw a relative who had left the hut and come across land where the river looped back on itself.

Dayuma beached the canoe and anxiously asked for news of her family. The woman did not know what had happened to Akawo, but she described in graphic detail the bloodbath in the hut. She described how she had found Nimu hacked to pieces on the dirt floor. Many women and children had been killed that night by Moipa who had had the strength of several men.

'He was mad,' she said, simply.

Dayuma decided that she had to return and find out for herself the fate of her mother. She could not leave the Land not knowing if she were dead or alive.

The woman climbed into the canoe and the party turned back. It had taken them a matter of hours to reach that point, but now it was to take them five days to return. The strong current was against them, and they had only bamboo poles, not paddles, to control their craft. They stopped constantly at every bend to plunge into the jungle to search for signs of Akawo, who could be anywhere.

Dayuma knew that her mother would not return to her house for many days.

On the fifth day, Dayuma spotted her mother's footprint on a beach. To outsiders, all prints look the same, but to the Wagrani, every print was distinctive. That was how they knew who was where and with whom when travelling the trails. Dayuma followed her mother's trail until she caught up with her. Her first thoughts were for her father. What had happened to him?

'He was wounded badly in the knees,' Akawo said. 'We broke the spears off; that caused him much pain, but we could not pull them out, and we could not push them through. He had a spear in each leg. It was very bad.'

'And then?'

'And then he knew he would never walk again, so we buried him and he died. In the morning he died. It took him a long time.'

They knew Caento was dead, although he was under the ground, when his groans ceased. The dead were buried bound in a curled position, but the living were buried flat on their backs and covered with bamboo slats on which earth was piled. The groans of the dying could be heard until their air gave out.

Dayuma found it difficult to believe that her father was dead. He had cared for her all her short life. He knew everything: where the best food was, where the rivers were good to fish, how to build, how to make, which trail led where.

'I am going to the outside, Mother,' she said presently. 'Why don't you come with me? It is not safe for you to stay here alone. You know that Moipa will kill you.'

But Akawo would not go. The jungle was her home. In one day she had lost a husband, a father and a child. She would stay where they were buried.

Dayuma's cousin, Umi, had been with Caento when he had been attacked, and she was with Akawo now. She said she would go with Dayuma.

The Quichua girl Aepi had also been with Caento. Since the time he had rescued her from the river, she had scarcely left his side. Now her protector was gone, she also would go with Dayuma to return to her own people.

The others who had originally travelled with Dayuma decided they would remain in the land they knew. It was better than the place they did not know, although Aepi had told them about her childhood, and had assured them that the outsiders were not cannibals.

So it was that a party of three lonely girls set off down the river into an unknown life.

6

Rachel Meets Dayuma

DAYUMA ARRIVED AT THE HACIENDA ILA, after a journey of several months, in the summer of 1947. It was in this same summer that Rachel Saint, thousands of miles away in New Jersey, had the strong conviction that now was the time for her to make a fresh attempt to become a missionary. It took a year for her plans to reach fruition, so it was not until the following summer that she was a student in language school in Oklahoma. Most people would put these dates down to coincidence; Rachel had the assurance that it was a further example of the will of God working in a mysterious way.

During her journey, Dayuma had seen many strange things. She had tasted salt and rice and sugar for the first time. She had been offered, and had rejected, cigarettes. She felt strange in clothes, and uncomfortable under blankets. She had ridden in motor cars, and had nearly fainted with fear when confronted by a horse.

Of all the new things, the horse, a huge black animal bigger than anything in the jungle, was the most terrifying. The size of it, the feet of it, the teeth of it, were all too much for the girl and she closed her eyes and waited to be devoured.

After the horse, she decided, she would accept any fresh horror.

There were no more.

Don Carlos Sevilla greeted her with kindness and with interest. Aepi acted as interpreter for her and for Umi, who was so shy that she scarcely lifted her head. Don Carlos Sevilla, a courtly and old-world Spaniard, had been an early pioneer in Wagrani territory. He had had cotton and rice plantations at the

Hacienda Capricho on the upper Curaray in 1914, but constant battle with the Wagrani had finally defeated him. At one point, in 1918, his entire work force was massacred during his absence. He moved out of Wagrani territory to Hacienda Ila on the upper Napo, but still continued his trips into their land. He admitted frankly that by then the Wagrani fascinated him and he had an obsession to meet them in friendship. All he ever got, however, was their spears. He had had many narrow escapes.

What always puzzled him about the Wagrani was their total unpredictability.

At certain times of the year, Quichuans travelled deep into Wagrani territory on fishing trips and were never attacked. They fished, smoked their catch and returned unmolested. At all other times they were attacked by a hail of spears.

Dayuma fled from Moipa during one of these truce periods, and soon came across a large group of Don Carlos Sevilla's Indians collecting rubber, and fishing. Don Carlos had given orders that any Auca found by them was to be treated with consideration, so the three girls were given men's clothes and food. An Indian was sent upstream past the old Hacienda Capricho to inform the *patrón*. After two months, the large party returned upriver, past Dayuma's home. She and the other two girls were quiet in the canoe, and looked nervously at every bend, a favourite ambush spot. Two moons had passed since her father's death and since she had left her mother, but fear of Moipa was still great in her, and although so close to her home she had no desire to return.

The moment passed. They reached the Oglán which flowed into the Curaray high upstream where the jungle trail from Shell Mera to Arajuno crossed.

Don Carlos Sevilla was waiting for them, with fresh clothes. This was the first white man that Dayuma had ever seen. He was tall, and spare-framed. His eyes were blue, a characteristic of many of north Spanish stock. 'How can the sky be in his eyes?' Dayuma asked Aepi.

The large Hacienda Ila was a source of fresh surprise. The log-walled main house was solid and spacious, filled with dark, heavy, Spanish colonial furniture, and woven rugs of intricate design were on the beeswaxed boards. There were dark oil paintings in gilt frames.

Dayuma was fascinated by a sombre painting of Don Carlos's mother. The fine aristocratic face looked out of the frame and into the distance. Round her neck was painted a necklace of large ingots of gold. It took some time for the young Indian girl to grasp the idea of the transference of images.

The girls were put to work on the plantation and lived with other workers in rough shacks. Their day was long, and routine did not come easily to them.

After a month on the hacienda, Dayuma's astonishment was extreme when her step-grandmother, Ominia, and another young relative, Winaemi, were brought in from the Oglán by rubber collectors.

'Your mother waited and watched for your return,' Ominia said. 'For three moons she waited, but still you did not come. She walked every day in the jungle looking for your trail, but saw nothing. Then she asked us if we would go to the outside to look. We said we would go quietly to the huts of the foreigners and watch. If we saw you, we would take you back.'

Ominia, Winaemi and her mother left with Akawo's instructions:

'Look well for my daughter. If she has been devoured by a jaguar, find her bones. If she is on the outside, see her. Bring me any news.'

They followed the downriver route taken by Dayuma and came across a Yumbo hunting party. Winaemi's mother instantly dived into the river and made for the opposite bank where she leapt through the undergrowth. Ominia and Winaemi showed more courage. They approached the strangers and asked them about Dayuma. They were given food and shelter for the night. The strangers chatted away to them, and the two Wagranis questioned them back, but there was no real communication. When the Yumbos attempted to take them to Hacienda Ila, there had been no resistance.

'But now you are here, and still my mother doesn't know,' Dayuma said. 'And now also, Winaemi's mother doesn't know.'

They discussed escaping back to the jungle, but although Don Carlos Sevilla was more considerate of his workers than most *patróns*, he still believed all Indians to be not far removed from wild animals, and the girls were under constant observation. They did, in fact, make three attempts at freedom over the years, but were quickly brought back.

It was not long before Aepi was taken to Quito as a maid-servant in Don Carlos Sevilla's town house. She was delighted, and became an avid cinemagoer. She also made quick friends with Joaquina who had been given to Don Carlos by her original *patrón*, Sam Souder, who had taken her to the Buen Pastor nunnery in Quito as an interpreter two years previously in 1946. Aepi forgot all her Wag in a very few months. Joaquina, being older, remembered the language a little longer, and for this reason was introduced to Rachel Saint.

A Swedish writer and explorer, Rolf Blomberg, came to the Hacienda Ila on the Anzu River in 1949 on his way into Wagrani territory. He was travelling with an adventurous Columbian photographer, Horacio Lopez, who for some reason called himself 'Robinson'. In their party also was a missionary, David Cooper, from Hollywood. 'Probably the only one Hollywood has ever produced', as Blomberg put it.

Blomberg wanted to meet the Aucas as he was writing a book about them. In fact his book, *The Naked Aucas*, is about his attempts to meet them, since the nearest he came to doing so was a spear attack launched by Moipa on the Nushino, a river which flows north of, and parallel to, the Curaray.

Blomberg met Dayuma and the other Wagrani at the Hacienda Ila. He said they were working well and seemed settled, with no desire to return home. Don Carlos Sevilla's eighteen-year-old son, Vicente, acted as interpreter between the Wagrani and Blomberg's party. Dayuma had learned to speak Quichuan, and Vicente communicated with her in this language, translating into Spanish for Blomberg.

Blomberg had the bright idea of taking one of the Aucas with him as an interpreter, and Vicente wanted to accompany them. Don Carlos Sevilla refused both requests. He said the proposed expedition was too small and vulnerable. Blomberg could kill himself if he wished, but not his son.

As Blomberg and his party travelled, they repeated aloud phrases they had picked up phonetically from Dayuma; phrases which they hoped would help when they met their first Auca.

In his diary for Tuesday, 29 March 1949, Blomberg wrote: 'Have never seen more abundant animal life anywhere in Oriente than here around the Nushino. Crocodiles, huge lizards, terrapins; five charapa terrapins lay sunning themselves on a log, all five dived into the river as on a word of command at our approach; a comical sight! Otters, agoutis, monkeys of different kinds, parrots, toucans, duck, egrets, and the most wonderful butterflies. Fantastic! The sort of thing one reads about and never believes!'

They stopped for the night on a sand playa. Blomberg wrote:

The howling monkeys had their skin singed off and were smoked. They are horrible to look at, like sooty devils. Cooper examined the paujil birds' crops in the hopes of finding lumps of gold, with poor results.

Quite a lot of mosquitoes here. No sleep for either the Indians or Robinson, but Cooper is sleeping like a log. A crocodile is swimming to and fro in the river. Its eyes shine like rubies when we turn the light on it. It is a good sentry. So long as it stays in the river no Aucas will come wading up . . .

The reference to the paujil birds is interesting. There were many stories of gold in the rivers, although not many people had actually stayed long enough to find it. Don Emilio Vega was an Oriente veteran who had spent nearly fifty years in the jungle, and had some lively stories to relate. He described how a captured Auca woman had told her *patrón* as long ago as 1909 that there was 'masses' of gold in a gully near her home on the Shiripuno, but they had no interest in it. It could not be eaten, or used to make tools. It was not even decorative. Don Emilio himself had frequently found gold, though not while panning for it. 'That's a fool's game,' he said. He had found small nuggets in the crops of paujil birds he had shot for meat.

On the seventh day in Wagrani territory, Blomberg's party knew for certain they were being followed.

'What we saw really convinced us that we were dealing with cunning savages, and savages probably on the war-path. In order to leave no visible tracks, they had not walked on the sandy shore, but in the shallow water, each man stepping in the footmarks of the man before him. It was therefore impossible to say how many had passed that way,' said Blomberg.

Ten minutes later the party, on two separate rafts, came under a hail of Auca spears. Ignoring the crocodiles they had recently passed, Cooper and Robinson dived into the water. Blomberg kept his head and fired round after round from his old Browning into the tall bamboo lining the river.

The Aucas had chosen the ideal spot in which to ambush them. A fallen tree had blocked most of the river, and the rafts had to steer right into the bank where a hand-held spear could almost touch them. In spite of this, the only injury received by a member of their party was a spear wound in the foot of one of the Yumbos. Blomberg attributes this to the fact that they had surprised the Aucas before they were properly in position, and his rapid firing had driven them off.

They climbed ashore and hunted about for a sign. They found plenty of tracks, bloodstains, and 'eight beautiful spears adorned with feathers'.

After a brief discussion, the three men decided there was no point in continuing their search to make contact with the Aucas – contact of a friendly nature, that is. Their few Auca expressions such as 'we are your friends' no longer meant very much in the context of their recent battle.

They made their way back to the Hacienda Ila, where Dayuma exclaimed over the spears. They were Moipa's, she said. He made his in such a way, using the feathers in a distinctive pattern.

Evidence that Moipa was still there, and still in a fighting frame of mind, convinced her that it was too dangerous for her to return, and she gave herself over entirely to becoming a civilized Quichua. She grew out her traditional fringe to cover the large holes in her ear lobes, and she began to forget her language. When the local Roman Catholic missionary came to the hacienda to teach, Dayuma listened, and soon she was christened. Her new name was Catherine.

Rachel Saint and the Wycliffe have always in the past been given the credit of converting Dayuma. Much was made of this on Ralph Edward's *This Is Your Life* television show featuring Rachel on 5 June 1957, and a great deal of publicity was given to Dayuma's public baptism on 15 April 1958, in Wheaton Evangelical Free Church, the local church of Wheaton College where Nate Saint had first enrolled. Rachel explains the discrepancy by saying that she never encouraged all the publicity; American evangelical organizations have huge public relations machines which are necessary to raise funds, but these are frequently 'the bane of a missionary's life. Personally I hate it'.

The difference between Dayuma's Roman Catholic baptism and her Protestant one, Rachel said, was that the first time round it was merely a matter of form, with no meaning, and the second time she had truly been saved. Therefore it had been accurate to tell the world that she was the first Auca Christian, and a product of Wycliffe's missionary work.

Dayuma had another reason for not wanting to return to the land of her ancestors: she was in love.

The object of her blossoming passion was Don Carlos Sevilla's son, Vicente. Marriage, of course, was out of the question. Lust was not, and in the summer of 1952 Dayuma gave birth to a son whom she called Ignacio.

Ignacio was something of an embarrassment to Don Carlos. Dayuma soon found herself the possessor of a respectable dowry, and a Quichuan husband, Miguel Padilla, who took his bride, her child, and her dowry to a Quichuan settlement owned by Don Carlos Sevilla on the upper Curaray.

A year later, Dayuma had another son. Shortly after his birth an outbreak of measles, to which Amazon Indians have no resistance, swept through the settlement. Miguel Padilla died, and Dayuma, burning with fever, crawled on her hands and knees to bury him. When the new baby also died, she was too ill to move. All her hair fell out, and she lay on her mat with a dead baby on one side, and a very sick Ignacio on the other. Eventually a neighbour found them and buried the baby beside his father. For the first time in her life Dayuma considered suicide, but she was too ill to drag herself to the river where she hoped to drown.

Ignacio recovered and Dayuma pulled herself together in order to care for him. There is nothing more insistent than a demanding child. She decided to return to the Hacienda Ila where she was given a home with Miguel Padilla's aunt, Olimpia, and it was not long before she was back at work from dawn to dusk working for her *patrón*, grandfather of her son.

When Rachel Saint and Catherine Peeke arrived at the Hacienda Ila in a Wycliffe float-plane in February 1955, at the invitation of Don Carlos Sevilla, Ignacio Padilla was three years old. Rachel was not very enthusiastic about the name; it smacked of Catholicism, and if there was one thing Rachel Saint did not like, it was the Roman Catholic Church.

She called the boy Samuel Padilla. Sam.

7

Sam's Childhood on the Hacienda

SAM'S VERY FIRST MEMORIES go back to about his third year, to the dark of the morning in Olimpia's thatch hut as Dayuma rose and fumbled in the gloom to dress herself and take some food before leaving for the planted fields.

The jungle was a constant enemy, but Don Carlos Sevilla with his large work force had managed to keep it at bay and to carve out order from the wilderness. His own house was probably the only substantial two-storeyed building in the Oriente. It was big and rambling, with many rooms for the family, and for the travellers who were always passing by. It was a jungle tradition to have open house at all times. There were frequently so many guests that Don Carlos had built several small guest houses, and these, with the outside kitchens that provided the workers' meals, the workers' houses, store sheds and even a school for the hacienda children, gave the whole place the air of a feudal estate.

The cleared fields stretched into the distance – banana, maize, rice, yucca, and cotton, divided by palm and fruit trees. There were horses and cattle. The river rushed by the massive log house, and there were many canoes at a constructed landing stage.

The hacienda was cut off from the world by a rough jungle trail over which it was impossible to drive, but Don Carlos Sevilla was taking care of this problem by building an airstrip. Towards this he had brought up a great deal of the equipment from the abandoned Shell Oil camp at Arajuno. Had Moipa been aware of it, he would have been able to congratulate himself for the responsibility of driving Shell away; a company which had invested millions of pounds in exploration fifteen years before any other company, and which had been chased out of a region rich in oil by a handful of Indians. The implications were staggering. In fact, Shell never regained an interest in the Oriente, and the vast profits today from the oil of Ecuador are shared by Texaco–Gulf and CEPE, the Ecuadorian State Oil Company. Almost certainly Rachel Saint's civilizing influence on the Curaray and Tiwaeno was responsible for the breakthrough. Even the Japanese have a foothold in the ambitious pipeline which goes from the Amazon basin over the soaring peaks of the Andes, down to the Pacific coast to the refineries of Esmeraldas – a monumental engineering achievement.

When Don Carlos Sevilla had constructed the airstrip, it was the job of the smaller children to keep the grass short. Sam rose with his mother then, at about four or five o'clock, and while she went in one direction to the fields, he would go to the airstrip with a machete nearly as big as himself, and cut grass. It made fodder for the horses and cows. At the age of four or five he led the huge animals that still terrified his mother to the river to water them, and stood on a high box to groom the household riding horses. Then he would drive the cows to new pastures, and returning then to the hacienda, collect the eggs laid during the morning in any place but the nesting boxes constructed for that purpose. The work was hard, but enjoyable. None of the children was paid and the adult workers were certainly not paid their worth. But they got their keep and protection, and it was sufficient for them.

Sam was surrounded by animals, not only the domestic ones, but a large variety of jungle pets that were given to him. At different times during his childhood years he had monkeys, an ocelot, countless parrots, hawks and deer. There were wild rabbits, brown with white flashes, an ant-eater, turtle, and kinkajou (casumbo), the nocturnal honey bear. The animals and birds were well-loved while they were there, quickly forgotten when they died or escaped to the jungle.

As he grew older Sam was given dogs which he trained to hunt, and went into the jungle with the men and their sons. He had no father who recognized him, but in that community all the men were fathers to all the children.

Dayuma's day ended at eight or nine at night, long after it was dark. In the Amazon, night falls at about six in the evening, but there were indoor chores after the field-work was done. It was a hard life physically, far harder than the one she had been used to at home on the Curaray, but she grew to accept it.

Sam was happy as a child. He was never bored and never lonely, and now thinks that that way of life was an ideal existence for children.

'I never had that desire of wanting something else. We were told to work, so we did. That was okay. You don't have too many problems at that age.

We didn't grow up with toys, but who needs toys? We had real things. We had good times learning how to hunt and how to fish.'

Dayuma was no longer with her people, but she remembered their ways and tried to bring up her son in some of them. She swam with Sam as a baby, and when she judged he was old enough, she tossed him into a deep pool. He swallowed a great deal of water, then had no option but to swim for the bank, and she watched him, laughing. She was grown up now, with a child, but she could still swim like a fish, and she taught Sam all he needed to know about swimming under water, looking for the big fish that hid under stones, for the crayfish and the flat fish.

She was as quick and lithe as an otter, and Sam grew to be a strong swimmer. The best place to learn to swim is the river where there are quiet places and sandbanks, fast currents and whirlpools. Sam learned to handle all the different situations. His days were divided between work, which was good, and swimming, which was fun.

Sometimes there were punishments. The worst one of all was the hot pepper treatment. An old woman, a Záparo, nearly the last of her tribe, had wandered out of the jungle, and was living on the hacienda. She was too old to work hard in the fields, and was used as a grandmother to take care of all the children. She knew the traditional ways.

When Sam behaved badly, she took a jaguar's claw and coated it with *aji*, the hot pepper sauce, the hottest in the jungle, and wiped it back and forth, one, two, under Sam's eyelids.

'You almost lose your mind,' Sam said. 'You can nearly go crazy with the pain. When they punish, they really punish.'

The Záparo woman later left the hacienda when the jungle reclaimed it after the death of Don Carlos Sevilla, and in time she turned up at Tiwaeno. She now lives on the Curaray with some of the Tiwaeno Wagrani. Today, she is the last Záparo. Since 1947 they have all gone but her.

One of Sam's big problems at the hacienda were the vampire bats. Olimpia's hut was simple in construction, and there was always a way for the bats to enter. Sam often awoke in the morning with his toes or his head bitten. He had many scars; the bites were deep, though nothing was felt at the time. The blood poured out and the bats lapped it up. They must have injected some anti-coagulatory factor into the bloodstream since Sam was often still 'bleeding all over the place' in the morning. He also declared that bats grew to recognize their favourite victim. The same person was bitten time and time again, whilst others on the same straw mat were left alone.

'One bat takes a taste for your blood, and then you get no peace.' He said that there were about nine different kinds of vampire bat, of which only one variety drinks human blood.

Dayuma used a common toughening-up method on Sam, which modern child psychologists would not approve. She would take him into the jungle and dump him, telling him that she was leaving him there for the jaguars or anacondas, painting a lurid picture of what he could expect at their mercy, and then walk away. She told him those horrible stories in the belief that the more scared a child was, the braver he became. It seemed to work with Sam. Today he is scared of nothing.

Sam remembers the arrival of Rachel Saint and Catherine Peeke, partly because float-planes were uncommon, and the arrival of one at the hacienda caused a stir; but he remembers them chiefly because they 'grabbed all the kids and hauled them into the schoolhouse'.

Sam was one of the little fish caught in their net, and his education at the hands of Rachel Saint began. Bible stories flowed from the two women like a torrent, and all the children, as well as their parents, when they had the time, were captivated. Many of the stories they had already heard from the visiting Roman Catholic priests, but this was different. Here were two bright young women, totally interested in their audience, and giving them their constant attention.

'I don't think any of us looked on the stories as Bible stories,' Sam said. 'They were told in quite an exciting way, and we were all suckers for stories. We loved them. We didn't get too many stories in the jungle, and our minds were wide open to receive anything that was new. In the city, it's right the opposite. You can't get a kid to Sunday school. We went willingly.'

Of his mother, Sam said: 'She was just like a regular Quichuan then, you know? Messing about and so on. That's how I came out. Then the missionaries came and she got changed and got into good habits.'

Rachel's meeting with Dayuma was, in its way, an historic event.

Inevitable changes in the Oriente accelerated from that date. Rachel had no doubt that the events of her life had led her up to that point. Had she left to work with the Aucas sooner, before Dayuma was out of the jungle waiting, unbeknown to herself, to take the missionaries back in with her, the chances are that she would have been killed as everyone else had been who attempted to go in.

'That was a sweet little thing from the Lord,' Rachel said, 'because if we had heard about them earlier, there would have been a very grave question as to whether we had any right to stay there; but we didn't hear about it until the danger was past. These people had speared any foreigner who entered their territory before we went in there, and we were the first outsiders ever to survive in Auca territory.'

Rachel found it incredible that, at last, after so many years of waiting and planning, she was actually talking to a real live Wagrani.

Dayuma's companions, Umi, Ominia, and Wiñaemi, had forgotten their language, but Dayuma still knew a few words. Rachel hoped that by patient encouragement, Dayuma would remember more. She believed that the fact that she herself knew no Quichuan, and so could not converse on any common level with Dayuma, would be an asset. Had she been able to speak Quichuan, as Catherine Peeke could, she thought that Dayuma would fall back on the easiest way out and not exert her mind.

At the Summer Institute of Linguistics they called this method 'ye olde monolingual approach'. It involved acting out pantomimes and pointing to objects, and Dayuma threw herself into the game with energy and child-like amusement. At times, Rachel found the fact that Dayuma was still employed as a full-time *peon* (labourer) very frustrating. Days passed and the most she would see of Dayuma was her distant figure working in the fields, or returning late at night too exhausted to want to work on language studies.

As a guest of Don Carlos Sevilla, who showed them great consideration, Rachel could not distract Dayuma from her duties by chatting with her as she worked in the fields.

Rachel and Catherine ate their meals with the Sevilla family at the long polished dining-table. The food was excellent and they were waited on by quiet, well-trained house-girls. Their room was on the first floor of the hacienda, lit by flickering oil lamps. Bed linen was crisp and starched, floors were waxed, cutlery polished, and the whole place run like a well-organized hotel.

During the day, Rachel and Catherine taught in the school or wrote up their language notes, struggling to make sense of the few words remembered by Dayuma. The words were few, but by the end of a month, Rachel's phonetic list was far longer than any collected over the years from all sources, including that of the German anthropologist, Gunter Tessman, published in 1930. By the end of the second month, the brief evening sessions had produced whole sentences. Rachel could see Dayuma struggling to remember, her mouth shaping the sounds over and over again as she frowned in perplexed concentration. She would spend the lonely day in the fields trying to remember, digging back into a past she had tried to forget; the past of a jungle and a family she had loved, but a past that had been filled with the horror of Moipa, and savage killings.

It seemed incredible to Dayuma, as she looked about her at the peaceful, ordered hacienda, that just a few miles away her people were living and killing. The memories invoked by Rachel's careful questions raised a storm of anxiety in Dayuma. The fears of her childhood years, the panic of her traumatic escape from the jungle, the homesickness she had tried to forget, all came to the surface of her clouded mind, and when she remembered, she broke down. She trembled with fury and passion as she thought of Moipa, and she wept for her lost relatives. She began to drink heavily, and begged Don Carlos Sevilla to give her a gun so that she could go and kill Moipa and avenge her father's death.

Rachel was startled by the Pandora's Box she had inadvertently opened. 'But I believe she had to get it all out of her system,' she said. 'She could not be cleansed and made whole with all that hatred in her.'

Another blow fell: Olimpia died, and Dayuma gave up her evening conversations with Rachel. She was too drunk. It was a very bad time, but Rachel went to Dayuma's hut to try to get through to her. Don Carlos Sevilla was more firm. He ordered Dayuma to pull herself together. Between the two of them, Dayuma resumed interest in her language lessons, and now her passion was spent, the language progressed rapidly. Rachel learned a great deal about the Aucas, preparing herself for the day when she would go and live with the tribe. She found that much of Tessman's information about the tribe, gathered from a variety of informants, was inaccurate. Dayuma was a valuable source of information.

In June 1955, Rachel had to leave the hacienda. Months of illness followed. She did not know it, but in her absence Jim Elliot, one of the missionaries working in association with Nate Saint, was visiting Dayuma to gather language information from her.

Nate Saint, Jim Elliot, Roger Youderain, Ed McCully and Pete Fleming, with their wives and small children, all lived in various places originally started as Shell Oil camps, in the area between Shell Mera in the south, and the Napo River further north. Jim Elliot and his wife, Elisabeth, lived at Shandia only four hours away across the jungle trail from the Hacienda Ila.

As Blomberg had done a few years previously to aid him in his approach to the Aucas, Jim Elliot hiked to the hacienda to collect a basic word list from Dayuma.

The reason he wanted this list and why Nate Saint's sister Rachel knew nothing about it, was that the five men had decided they would make a breakthrough and make contact with the Aucas, but they did not want to tell anyone because they knew there would be a great deal of opposition to this dangerous course.

Their wives, of course, knew. Nate Saint, Jim Elliot and Ed McCully, the three men originally involved, called their plan *Operation Auca*, and it took shape in September 1955, three months after Rachel had left Hacienda Ila.

Sam and Dayuma remember seeing the little yellow Piper Comanche constantly flying over the hacienda as Nate Saint searched the rivers flowing east for signs of Auca houses. Had Rachel still been there, she would have been very curious about the flurry of activity in the sky. She would have guessed the reason and, in her determined way, would have caused the fur to fly.

But she was not there, and was to know nothing about it until all five men had been killed, and by then, the whole world knew.

8

Death of the Five Missionaries on 'Palm Beach'

NO ONE KNOWS WHY the men went in when they did. Nate Saint knew of Rachel's obsessive interest in the Aucas, and they all knew she was working with Dayuma and building up a good vocabulary. The vocabulary that Jim Elliot had gleaned was limited, and Dayuma could have given him reason to pause, with her vivid descriptions in Quichuan of her tribe's wild ways. None of the five had any reason to suppose that the Aucas had changed their spots.

The simple fact is that they all had faith. Faith that anything they did was the will of God if it went against them; a miracle, if it turned out well. Either way, the responsibility was not theirs.

Evangelists live through God. They shift all the responsibility for their actions on to him. If things are bad, it is his will and they pray for help, for understanding of the deeper meaning in his apparent turning away from them. If things are good, they rejoice, filled with the assurance that they are lifted up in his hands.

No one can argue with this logic, since in either way, they are right, and as in all things, it is a matter of being a believer or a disbeliever.

If you are a believer, you *know*; if a disbeliever, you need to be saved, to be rid of the Devil who casts doubt in your mind, and then you will know.

The five men knew that God wanted them to make contact with the Aucas. They made their plans carefully, and did not rush in like fools.

Nate Saint had invented a basket drop; a tin kettle which contained many gifts was lowered on a long line. Once the Auca houses had been located, he flew over and lowered his gifts, at the same time calling out the words of friendship and encouragement that Jim Elliot had learned from Dayuma.

Nate Saint kept a careful record of their motives and aims. He wrote: '6 October 1955. The first gift was a small aluminium kettle with a lid. Inside we put about twenty brightly-coloured buttons – obviously not for their non-existent clothes! But buttons do make good ornaments. Also we included a little sack with a few pounds of rock salt. We understand they do not have any salt of their own. If only they could discover what the salt was good for, we felt sure we'd win friends . . .'

Several yards of brightly-coloured ribbon streamers were attached to the kettle.

Nate Saint took off with Ed McCully for the Auca houses. They decided to drop their present on a beach close to one of the houses. In case they had to make a forced landing, the river was the safest place.

'. . . there was our messenger of good-will, love and faith, 2000 feet below us on the sand-bar. In a sense we had delivered the first Gospel-message-by-sign-language to a people who were a quarter of a mile away vertically, fifty miles horizontally, and continents and wide seas away psychologically. The trip back to Arajuno was short and happy. Back home again, everybody who was in on the secret wanted to know if we had seen any Aucas. They were a little sceptical about anyone finding our gift when we confessed we hadn't seen a soul. Nevertheless, a start had been made.'

It was their plan to continue the drops every week until a regular pattern was established so that the Aucas would expect them and know that they left things in friendship.

'It was decided . . . to leave something different each week in order to work on their curiosity. We calculated that under the circumstances, sooner or later the hostile spirit would melt.'

Although their intention was to go every week, they were so keyed up that they went more frequently. As they anticipated, the Indians had grown to expect them, and were always waiting *en masse* when the aeroplane flew overhead.

On one occasion, Nate Saint could not make up his mind at which house to leave the gift, and he reported that the whole group at one house charged off downriver to where he was then circling. When he changed his mind and returned to the original house, they all charged back upriver. He had no way of knowing what they thought of the gifts, or under what system the gifts were allocated. It seems not to have occurred to any of the missionaries that bloodshed could have resulted over fights for possession, as had happened in the case of similar drops made by the Shell Oil Company as Christmas gifts to the

Aucas some years earlier. Men had killed each other for ownership of a machete.

'It is really great sport,' Nate wrote in his journal. 'We don't know whether or not they have any system for determining who gets the prize. But as long as the supply holds out, they should all keep encouraged.'

The men noticed that when one of their gifts landed in trees, the Aucas cut down the trees to reach the packages, decorated with streamers for easy recognition. It seemed to them to be a good idea to encourage more trees to be chopped down, in a straight line, so that the aeroplane could get in really close to the houses. Up to then, most of their activity had been over the river. With this in mind, they started to drop axe-heads and machetes.

The remarkable thing is that the men *were* aware of the trouble caused in the past over machetes and axes. Nate wrote on 14 October: 'We landed at Arajuno and began to prepare for the "drop", which was to be a new machete. We understand that these people have killed for machetes. That is, they have killed people working in the fields in order to steal their machetes or axes. It is easy to imagine the importance of such items among a stone-age people. We wrapped the blade in canvas so that no one would get hurt.'

From this note it is obvious that the men believed that by supplying tools they would lessen the need for the Aucas to steal from and kill outsiders for them. What they had no idea of was that the men *within* the tribe might kill each other for possession. The comment about wrapping the machete in canvas showed concern for the Aucas, not thoughtlessness, and no one can be blamed for ignorance.

They also dropped many items of clothing and reported that the people had started leaving off their 'uniform' (of nudity) to wear the store-bought clothes.

Nate wrote on 10 December, 'These fellows will be dressed like dudes before we get to see them on the ground'.

The Aucas started to exchange gifts, tying theirs on to the end of the long line when possible. The gifts were small, but were received with exultation by the missionaries. It was the sign they had been waiting and praying for. The first gift was a feather head-dress, and subsequent ones were reed combs bound with woven cotton, and more feather decorations. One week the missionaries lowered a live chicken; the following week the Aucas returned a red parrot in a small basket inside the white canvas sack in which the chicken had been dropped. They had even included a banana for the parrot, and judging from its chewed state, the parrot had enjoyed a meal while travelling under the aeroplane at sixty miles an hour on their return to Arajuno.

As December 1955 approached, the men were in mixed frames of mind about making an attempt to land to make closer contact. Jim Elliot and Nate

Saint were champing at the bit, Ed McCully was 'committed', Pete Fleming was 'vitally interested' but had not yet been given the go-ahead by God, and Roger Youderain was in the middle of a spiritual battle and had been planning to return home. He was despondent over his singular lack of success in saving souls amongst the Jivaros with whom he was working.

In a deeply depressed mood he wrote in his diary, 'About ready to call it quits. The reason: Failure to measure up as a missionary and get next to the people. Since March . . . there has been no message from the Lord for us. I wouldn't support a missionary such as I know myself to be, and I'm not going to ask anyone else to.'

None of the others knew about Roger Youderain's inner battle. When Nate Saint asked him if he would join their party, far from jumping at the chance to 'prove' himself, Roger prayed about it until he was certain that it was God's will, and not just a gimmick to give him a spiritual boost.

On 19 December 1955, shortly before the final trip to the Curaray, Roger Youderain wrote in his diary, 'I will begin to ask God to put me in a service of constant circumstances where, to live in Christ, I must die to self.'

Marilou McCully and her husband Ed were stationed at Arajuno, and on 11 December, Marj Saint heard over the radio at Shell Mera that Marilou, who was holding the fort alone, was certain that Aucas were around the air-strip at Arajuno. Marj called Nate who flew the few miles to Arajuno, first picking up Ed McCully who was at Puyupunga, a settlement located between the two stations.

Marilou was in the house with the local Quichuas, in the middle of a carol service, and it took some time persuading the Indians to leave. They were given candy to help the spirit of bravery, and were told that if there were Aucas about, then it would be good if they could do a little missionary work themselves. The Quichuas were not convinced of this, but took the candy and left.

Marilou was obviously very nervous; the last Auca raid in Arajuno had left a number of dead bodies lying around riddled with spears.

Ed was relaxed and said laconically, 'Now get hold of yourself, lady. Everything's going to be okay. All we want are the facts.'

Marilou's nerves were obviously a reaction to a small act of courage on her part. Ed was rather startled when she told him that after definite Auca footprints had been found leading up to the house, she had headed down the runway bearing a machete as a gift, calling out in Auca, 'I like you, I like you'.

Behind her, the Indian guard was calling from a safe distance, 'You're crazy, they'll kill you'.

When Marilou found a fresh wet footprint on the path, she tossed the machete on the path and slowly retreated; she was seven months pregnant.

The two men took over. They adorned themselves in some of the gift feather head-dresses, and decorated a new aluminium kettle with coloured ribbons as a sign of recognition, then strolled down the runway, calling out their Auca phrases. Nothing happened. They repeated this exercise later in the day looking, as Nate said, 'Like a couple of Don Quixotes in the role of Santa Claus delivering goodies to the trees'.

Again there was no response, so Nate and Ed McCully decided to fly over the Auca settlement in the evening and make their gift drop. They did so and saw no men, only women, which convinced them that there had, indeed, been a visit to Arajuno in force. Their gift contained packages of food wrapped in banana leaves, beef, chocolate, yucca, cookies, candy, and some beads. They received a gift back, tied to the end of the line, of a large black bird in a basket-cage, and a piece of bark-cloth (probably a wild turkey).

On 23 December they made another flight to drop gifts, and went down very low. They saw an older man, whom they had frequently seen at a distance, and who had shown little interest in them, unlike some of the others who had waved and shouted and climbed trees to get a closer look.

'Wow!' Jim Elliot said. 'That man's scared stiff.'

Although he was piloting the aeroplane, Nate Saint had also seen the Auca's expression, and he agreed. He said the people tried to appear friendly, probably in order not to discourage the gifts, but their eyes were full of terror.

The gifts they dropped included a flashlight. 'What wouldn't we give to see them trying to make sense out of that flashlight!' wrote Nate.

The Aucas signalled that they had a gift to send back and they held up a package. It felt very heavy on the end of the specially designed spiralling line when it was fixed in place. On their return to Arajuno, the men let it down too quickly and it landed hard. The package contained cooked fish, small leaf-wrapped packets of peanuts, two pieces of cooked yucca, a cooked plantain, two squirrels (apparently killed by the hard fall), one live but nervous parrot and two bananas for it, two shattered clay pots, a piece of cooked meat, and a smoked monkey tail. The Aucas were giving all they had to give, a remarkable gesture from people who had so little in material things.

It looked, however, as if the secret was out. Some of the Quichuas asked why they were wasting good gifts on no-good Aucas, and later, other Quichuas

TOP: Nate Saint, Naenkiwi ('George') and Roger Youderain on 'Palm Beach' on the Curaray, scene of the massacre of the five missionaries two days later. Although the Wagrani hate anything savoury, Naenkiwi is eating a hamburger with mustard, while Roger applies insect repellent. BOTTOM: Gimari ('Delilah') on Palm Beach, Dayuma's younger sister, it was her runaway affair with Naenkiwi which led to the massacre. Note the balsa plugs in the ears.

from Arajuno, on a short trip down the Curaray, stripped off, quickly cut long sticks to look like lances, and pranced about naked on a *playa* when they heard the aeroplane, hoping that some of the gifts would come their way.

The missionaries decided that the time was ripe for them to make an attempt to land in Auca territory. Nate found a long beach on the Curaray which he had not seen before, the river having dropped considerably. He tested the length by dropping bags of coloured powder paint and eventually made his first landing on the *playa* which they humorously referred to by the code name of 'Palm Beach', although it was a far cry from the Miami playground.

The date was 2 January 1956.

They saw no sign of the Aucas, the *playa* being some distance from their houses, but they examined the site and calculated where they would build a tree-house in which they intended to live for the first few weeks of their contact in case of flooding, and they planned to cut down a few trees to make it safer for landing and take-off.

Tinted self-portraits had been taken of them all, wearing gift head-dresses and holding Auca combs. They glued the blown-up prints to boards, sketched the aeroplane in each corner as a recognition signal, and dropped the five photographs during one fly-over. Nate reported that the Aucas had opened the package, and all of them had clustered around. He said he wished he knew what they were saying, but at least the Aucas had seen their pictures, and if they met on the beach on the Curaray, the men thought they would recognize them as being the same people who had dropped gifts over so many weeks.

They discussed the Aucas who had visited Arajuno so recently. There had been no bloodshed then; just a quiet look. They reviewed the gifts, and the approaches by Aucas who had built platforms high in the trees as if to get closer to the plane. They had seen spears only once, so it did not look as if the men were on the warpath. The unusually long sandy beach, which had not been there before, seemed designed just for them by divine intention. The rains would come in a month and then the river would flood, and it would be too late. They reviewed all these facts, and then prayed. They said that if at any time there had been a sign from God that they were not intended to make the attempt, they would have stopped at once. According to them, no such sign came, and they took this to mean that their mission was blessed.

Nate Saint wrote: 'As we weigh the future and seek the will of God, does it seem right that we should hazard our lives for just a few savages? As we ask ourselves this question, we realize that it is not the call of the needy thousands,

News of the massacre travelled around the world, arousing enormous interest and concern. The 'savage Aucas', again, had lived up to their fearsome reputation. The search party discovered all the men, their bodies still riddled with spears. They are buried on 'Palm Beach' not far from where today Dayuma and her group live in peace

rather it is the simple intimation of the prophetic Word that there shall be *some from every tribe in His presence on the last day* and in our hearts we feel that it is pleasing to Him that we should interest ourselves in making an opening into the Auca prison for Christ.'

On 6 January 1956, all the men were in place, waiting on the sandbank on the Curaray. It was hot and the flies bothered them. Jim Elliot stood in the shallows, his phrasebook in hand, shouting out welcoming sentences to the impassive trees. Roger Youderain imitated him off the centre of the bank, and Ed McCully went to the top end.

Suddenly a deep Auca voice boomed out from the trees, and a man appeared with two women, one about thirty, and one about sixteen. The man pointed to the girl and said something. The missionaries thought he was probably offering her in trade, and they jokingly nicknamed her 'Delilah'.

The Aucas made gestures and it seemed that they wanted one of the missionaries to go across to their side of the river. Jim Elliot began to wade across.

'Be careful,' he was warned.

He hesitated for a moment, then continued to the other side.

The Aucas seemed hesitant. Jim held out his hand, and Delilah stepped slowly off a log and came towards him and took his hand. The other two Aucas followed, and Jim took their hands to lead them over to the sandbank.

It had happened so suddenly that the five missionaries could not believe it was actually taking place after all their months of hope, and prayer, and planning, and after all the centuries of legend about these wild people.

Gifts were offered which were received 'with cries of delight'. The older woman leafed through *Time* magazine, while the man – they called him George – squatted on his haunches to eat a hamburger with mustard, while Roger rubbed him down with insect repellent.

Delilah drifted over to the aeroplane parked under the trees and rubbed herself along it, imitating a flying movement with her hands. 'She seemed dreamy', wrote Pete Fleming.

George approached the aeroplane and indicated that he wanted a ride. They put a shirt on him, since it was cold in the sky, and took off. They circled the beach, and he leaned out, shouting phrases to the ground in the same way as the missionaries had done during their many visits to the settlements. Nate landed on the beach, but George indicated that he wanted to go up again.

This time, Nate took him over the houses, and there was a great deal of communication between him and the people below.

An old woman looked astounded, and a young man who shinned up to the platform looked delighted.

When they returned again to the beach, George leaped out and clapped his hands. The missionaries promptly broke into prayer, their heads raised to the sky to show they were 'addressing their Heavenly Father'. George did not seem to be particularly impressed, and the missionaries felt greatly frustrated by their lack of communication.

They spent some time after prayers showing the three Aucas things like rubber balloons and a yo-yo. They had lemonade and more hamburgers with mustard, which were enjoyed. But all the time George seemed restless. He wanted to go up in the aeroplane again, and when the missionaries got in to make a flight themselves, George put in his gift packages, climbed in himself, and refused to leave. So up they went again in a repeat performance.

On their return they asked George if he would take them to the village, but he was either reluctant or did not understand. They asked him to get his group to cut down trees and build an airstrip, demonstrating by use of a model plane and twigs in the sand. They discovered that some of their pronunciations were wrong, and George put them right. They thought he understood what they meant about the airstrip, and once more gave thanks in prayer at their progress.

Meanwhile, Delilah was growing restless. She wanted to convey something, but the men did not understand her. When Jim Elliot headed for the tree-house, she jumped up to follow him eagerly, but when he turned back, she looked downcast.

Before nightfall, Nate Saint and Pete Fleming prepared to leave for the short flight to Arajuno. George understood that he was not to go with them, and the two Americans left. The three Aucas indicated that they would spend the night on the beach, and the remaining three Americans offered them the beach shelter they had built. George and the older woman squatted down, but Delilah seemed petulant about something and stalked off down the beach, with George following her. The older woman remained squatting by the fire, talking non-stop to Roger Youderain. When he wearily climbed into the tree-house, she remained on the beach chatting away to the stars for most of the night.

That night there were quiet celebrations back at Arajuno, Shell Mera, and Shandia among the wives and Nate Saint and Pete Fleming, who were all in communication by radio, using code words to keep the secret. In Shandia, where Rachel Saint was staying with Elisabeth Elliot while recuperating from her illness, the celebration was one of the spirit rather than physical, as the secret had to be kept, even from her.

The next day, Saturday, 7 January, after Nate Saint and Pete Fleming returned was one of tension and disappointment on Palm Beach. No one came. The men sat about all day, praying, reading in the water – a 'hydraulic siesta' to keep the flies off – and shouting phrases to the unresponsive jungle.

At four-thirty in the afternoon, Nate Saint and Pete Fleming circled the settlement. They were disturbed to see signs of fear, and some of the formerly friendly Aucas ran to hide. Nate threw them some shorts and a blanket, and called out 'Come, come, come!' before returning to the beach where they waited hopefully.

Later, they again flew over the settlement. This time, George appeared and smiled, and one old man pointed to Palm Beach and seemed 'friendly but not exuberant'.

Nate returned to the beach, hoping that the pointing had indicated a visit, but no one came so he took off for a third time. On this occasion the Aucas appeared to be more friendly, George smiled a great deal, and there were no longer any signs of fear. Even so, they did not pay a visit to the missionaries that night.

Nate Saint and Pete Fleming returned to Arajuno feeling more depressed than they had been when they had left the place earlier, but during the night, Nate felt his spirits rise again and by the morning was quite buoyant.

Marilou McCully had baked some fresh blueberry muffins which were still hot from the oven. She also packed ice cream in an ice box. 'It will still be cold when you get it to the beach,' she said. 'The others will enjoy a cool treat. Make sure you eat it up at once.'

Ed McCully grinned as he climbed into the plane. 'So long girls,' he called to his wife and to Marj Saint. 'Pray for us. I believe today's the day.'

The muffins were still warm and the ice cream still cold, and the men tucked into what was indeed a treat. They all felt excited. They had not been able to interpret what the lack of a visit by the Aucas the previous day had meant, but there had been no signs of hostility in the night. They were all certain that that day, Sunday, would be a very important one in their lives.

Nate finished his ice cream, they said a prayer, and then he took off to circle the settlement which they had code-named 'Terminal City'.

He could see only a few women and was convinced that the men must be on the trail towards the beach. He dipped the plane, and saw the Aucas in single file, heading for the river.

Nate landed on the beach as quickly as he was able, and shouted out, 'This is it, guys! They're on the way!'

It was then almost twelve-thirty, time for a radio contact with Marj Saint in Shell Mera.

His voice full of an excitement she could detect, Nate Saint told his wife, 'This is it. There's a commission of ten on the way from Terminal City. Looks like they'll be here for the early afternoon service. Pray for us. This is the day! We'll contact you again at four-thirty.'

9

The Massacre – the Wagrani Story

THE FOLLOWING INFORMATION WAS TOLD to Dayuma by her people in June 1958:

Wawae had been away hunting when Moipa had carefully chosen his moment to fatally wound Caento and kill many of Wawae's weaker relatives. By the time Wawae had returned, Dayuma had fled, and his mother had vanished.

Moipa thought he had influenced Wawae sufficiently to avoid a revengeful visit, but he was wrong. Traditional ways were deeply ingrained, and Wawae was wild with rage. He recalled a fact that most people in the tribe had forgotten; that Caento had taken in the orphaned Moipa and had raised him as a son in the days before he married Akawo and had other children.

Moipa had not killed an enemy but had turned, like the snake he was, on the man who was his foster-father.

Wawae and the members of his hunting party, absent at the time of Moipa's treachery, heard the story out, then cut new spears. As the weapons were prepared, their anger was fed, and as each point was sharpened, they described what they would do with it. Moipa was going to look like a porcupine if their threats had any weight.

When they arrived at Moipa's hut, he was not there. He had gone on a raid outside their land, Wawae was told. Wawae thought otherwise. 'He has run before our spears!' he yelled, and charged into the hut. 'He has killed our women, we will kill his.'

He had made so much noise about his intentions that the hut was nearly

86

empty, most of the occupants having fled from the rear exit. Moipa's wife, Tamaya, was still there with her little baby, and Wawae killed them both before his anger had cooled. Instead of killing the others he found cowering near by, he took them back to his clearing as prisoners. Included in this band of prisoners was Naenkiwi who had been trained as a killer, first by Aentyaeri in the days when Mingi had been killed, and then by Moipa. Wawae did not kill Naenkiwi because he was his cousin, and Naenkiwi's mother, who lived with Wawae, had begged him not to.

In order to prevent a counter-attack, Wawae cut a new trail in the jungle to make it look as if they had all fled to the outside when Moipa came looking for them; then the whole group moved deep into the interior.

Moipa and his group also moved a great distance from the Curaray in case Wawae and his supporters came after him, and for several years each group roamed the jungle many miles from their home on the Curaray, convinced that the other group was still there. During this period, the Curaray was nearly deserted. There was peace on the borders and the outsiders were thankful, although they could not understand the reason.

In time, both groups, now a long way downriver, drifted, unknown to each other, closer together. There was a wild Downriver group between them – a group to which they were all related, since every Wagrani is related to each other – whom they rarely saw, so deep in the interior did they live. This group made very rare contact with the outside, and consequently were more primitive, relying on stone axes for tools.

When Moipa eventually discovered that Wawae was living very close to him, he went to the men of the Downriver group who lay between him and his enemy, and made a pact with them that they would join forces to kill Wawae. Meanwhile Wawae, having discovered the whereabouts of Moipa, also went to the Downriver group and made a similar pact with them. The Downriver group, like all Wagrani having no sense of honour, agreed to help both sides.

Moipa was first to arrive, ready for battle against Wawae. The Downriver group immediately fell on him and his men and wiped them out. Moipa's head was severed from his body and daubed with decorative red achiote colouring, and hung up before his wife's gaze. She was now taken as wife by Warikona, one of the Downriver group. What Moipa had forgotten was that long ago he had speared the wife of Warikona, and had cut off her head and decorated it in the same manner, hanging it up on the trail for Warikona to find. Warikona's revenge was now complete.

All the women of Moipa's group were taken by the Downriver men, and for a short time were treated well. Then one of the women broke a large pot, and they were all speared to death with their children, except for Moipa's sister who, with her Downriver husband, Tuwa, fled. It is from these two that the full details are known.

Wawae was not aware of what was going on, and when the Downriver men eventually found his family group, he thought that they had come in peace, ready to cement the alliance.

Too late he realized his mistake and he was one of the first to fall, but several of his group escaped, one of whom was a four-year-old girl, Wato. The remnants of the group made their way upriver. After a month of wandering in the jungle, they found a trail littered with banana skins and half-chewed fruit. They followed the tracks and found Wato* lying wrapped in a vine thicket, shivering with fear, her bones showing gaunt through her once chubby body, and her hair fallen out. Minkayi, her uncle, claimed her. Her mother, Nombo, had been taken by the Downriver men.

They continued their journey upriver and soon discovered Akawo who had never strayed far from the Curaray. After her daughter Dayuma had fled to the outside, Akawo would not leave in case Dayuma returned. She made her home with her brother, Gikita, and, with the members of his family, made up the small house that remained in peace on the Curaray until the others returned.

The Curaray group grew in strength as more family members drifted back. The Wagrani have no routine about the jungle journeys they make. There is no particular time to live here or there, but they do tend to arrive in one area at round about the same time, often coming in from different directions in some sort of migratory pattern for which there is no apparent reason.

Suddenly their relative peace was shattered: a large 'wood-bee' began to fly overhead nearly every day. It circled, and swooped low, then circled again. They knew at once that it was watching them, looking for their houses. This had happened before in the past, but not with such frequency. The Wagrani clustered together, talking excitedly, discussing loudly with many gestures what they should do. There had been no killings on the outside for a long while; the outsiders were surely not coming in retaliation. They finally decided they would leave the river before they were raided.

Then one of the men came running from the river. He was carrying a small aluminium pot, bound with long coloured ribbons. They put it on the ground and looked at it, their voices rising and falling, the finder telling them, expressively, how the pot had come down from the sky from the wood-bee on the end of a long vine which dropped off after it. They looked at it with respect. It was a very long vine, and strong. It would be useful, and save them making

* Wato was later to marry Toña, the first Wagrani missionary.

more of their own for a while.

They liked the buttons inside the pot which were given to the children who at once threaded them and wore them, and they tentatively tasted the salt which they thought disgusting. They looked at it in some perplexity; clearly it was useful, but for what? They had no idea and threw it on one side. Within a few days the yellow wood-bee returned and there was another gift for them, a machete. They were very excited and talked wildly about who would take it. Gikita stepped forward. It had landed closest to his house; he would have it.

The next time the aeroplane came over, they were ready for it. They had seen people inside, who had waved and smiled, which confused them. How could people get inside a wood-bee? Discussions about the large flying insect and its contents were as vociferous as those about who was to have the gifts. At no time did any of them associate friendship with the men who flew in the plane. Some said they were devils, but others who had been to the outside and lurked in the bushes around the airstrip at Arajuno, said no, they were foreigners, not devils, though how they could ride in the body of the wood-bee, they did not know.

Their discussions continued hour after hour, day after day, but in their total ignorance of civilized things, the Wagrani could not possibly know the answer; everything was beyond their comprehension. Such is the huge gulf the missionaries and other outsiders must face when dealing with primitive people. Without language the civilized and the savage can have no communication on any footing but the most simple. Language is the key. The men who flew in the wood-bee did not have it. Their voices, echoing from the sky in competition with space and the noise of the plane, meant nothing at all. The Wagrani on the ground, straining to make sense of what they heard, were defeated by this and by incorrect pronunciation of the few words they managed to hear.

There were other problems about which the outsiders in their circling plane had no knowledge, but which were to play a crucial part.

Ever since Naenkiwi had been captured at spear-point from Moipa's hut when Wawae had gone to revenge his father's death, he had lived first with Wawae, then with Gikita and Akawo. During this period, some seven chonta seasons, he had grown in strength to full manhood. He had kidnapped his first wife after spearing her father to death, and this set the pattern of his life. When he wanted something, he took it. If he could not take it at once, he killed, and then took it. In this way he had acquired many wives in a group much reduced by years of killings. He even speared his own wives. He had killed his first wife when she protested that the girl he had snatched to be his second wife was too young.

When Naenkiwi turned his attention to her daughter Gimari, Akawo was furious. Gimari had been a child when Dayuma had run from the storm so long ago just before her father had died. She was a beautiful girl and Akawo decided that she would arrange a marriage for her with Dyuwi, the nephew of her sister-in-law, Gikita's wife. It was nearly in keeping with tradition, and Dyuwi was a handsome young man, strong, and without a wife.

A Wagrani marriage ceremony was simple and had an element of mystery about it. Everyone was in on the secret, except the bride. A party was organized, the men went to hunt and the women gathered fruit and made their un-fermented fruit *chicha* – a thick drink. The Wagrani frequently had feasts, so the bride had no reason to suspect anything. They had feasts when the crops were good, when certain fruit seasons came around, when there had been a very good hunt with big animals killed, when the fat monkey season was at its height – or just because they felt like one.

When the guests and the meal were ready, the dancing started and the moment was waited for when the bride was sitting alone in a hammock. If she sat when others in the know happened also to be resting there, they casually removed themselves, and the signal was given. Then the men raced up with the bride-groom and quickly sat him down next to the unsuspecting bride. One of the bride's male relatives, her father if he were alive, or a brother, was in the lead to 'give' the groom to her. Nothing more complicated than that took place, and the bride usually seemed to be quite happy with her elected partner. Love, *per se*, did not seem to enter very much into the picture, though no doubt desire did, and in such an incestuous community, was fulfilled regardless of who was officially married to whom.

So Akawo had decided that Gimari was to marry Dyuwi. But Naenkiwi had other ideas. As part of the male contingent he was informed about the forthcoming feast, and he grew jealous and possessive. He had several wives, but that did not stop him also wanting Gimari, and he arranged his own private bridal feast.

Events moved quickly and Naenkiwi's feast was well under way, the only people not in the picture about his intentions being Akawo's immediate family. Akawo suddenly woke up to the conspiracy half-way through the dancing as the party drew to its climax. She grabbed her daughter by the hand and they fled into the jungle, away from the houses, the flickering flames of the fire, and the chanting people. Akawo and Gimari built a rough shelter and slept out. They returned the next day and confronted a scowling, thwarted, would-be bridegroom.

Naenkiwi looked at the light of battle in Akawo's eyes, at her brother

Gikita, and at her son Nampa, who were holding their spears aggressively, and retired for the moment, though not admitting defeat.

Throughout all these manoeuvrings for possession of her, Gimari, who until that moment had not thought of marrying anyone, was seeing Naenkiwi with new eyes. As a warrior, he was something of a hero. He was a good deal older than she was, and he wanted her. It was enough; caveman tactics work as well in the jungle as anywhere else. She promptly decided she had lost her heart to him, much to her mother's disgust and her brother's anger.

In the middle of these affairs of the heart, the yellow wood-bee came with more offerings.

Life seemed to be growing very complicated for a group of uncomplicated people.

A chicken and some fluffy chicks were lowered from the sky. Nampa took care of these, and built a little house for them next to his own house. He thought that a return gift of a parrot might bring some other unusual foreign bird in return. By now, the Wagrani attitude was changing, as Nate Saint had forecast. They were growing curious and wanted to trade. They felt that so long as the foreigners stayed where they were, up in the sky, there was no danger.

Akawo had other ideas. Some of the gifts were good and valuable; axes, machetes, cooking pots that did not break. Her daughter, Dayuma, about whom she had thought constantly over the years, had gone to the outside, as her father, Caento, had told her. It occurred to Akawo that perhaps Dayuma had reached the outside, and that these gifts were from her to let her mother know that she was safe and well.

When a Wagrani died, he was dead. But when he went away and was lost, he was worried over. Without knowing the parable of the lost sheep, the Wagrani had all the sentiments of the shepherd.

Akawo related her thoughts to Nampa. 'I'll go up high into the trees and have a look,' he said. If Dayuma was in the wood-bee, he would see her. Wagrani had no idea of height or perspective. The plane could have been a hundred feet, or two thousand feet up. It was all the same; it was above the tree-tops.

Nampa built a small platform high in the trees and climbed up into it the next time the wood-bee came. It was no good. He could not see clearly the faces of those inside it. A trailing vine passed close to him and he caught at it and held on, but it snapped, fortunately for him, before he was very high off the platform.

The men in the aeroplane thought that the Aucas had built the platform to direct operations; they had no idea it was there to help Dayuma's brother to see his sister.

One day photographs were dropped. The Wagrani clustered around the strange objects. They saw the images of faces, of feather head-dresses, but they were meaningless. How could an image of a face, as seen in a stream, be a reflection of something that was not there? They looked up into the sky as they moved the large photographs about, but the reflections stayed the same. Where were they coming from? There was no one above. They did not associate the head-dresses with the gifts they themselves had returned to the wood-bee.

They turned their attention to a small piece of wood that had five notches cut in the side.

Dayuma had told Rachel Saint about the Auca carvings. Notches cut in trees in the jungle indicated direction or a message. Rachel Saint had grasped at the word, to describe her writing. She intended calling her Auca translations 'God's carving'. Dayuma had also described this system of simple communication to Jim Elliot, and the men had cut five notches in the piece of wood and sent it with the photographs – one notch for each man.

Akawo ignored the photographs, as the Wagrani do with anything they cannot comprehend, and she dived at the piece of wood.

'Five carvings,' she exclaimed. 'One each for my daughter Dayuma, Umi, Omiñia, Wiñaemi, and the little Quichua, Aepi. Surely the wood-bee is sent by Dayuma.'

Akawo was now convinced of this fact. She knew all foreigners were cannibals, but it was obvious to her that Dayuma lived and had not been eaten.

The Wagrani cannibal stories had been built up over the centuries from legend, based on fact, nourished by fear. It is very likely that lost travellers had eaten each other to survive. Long ago when old Karae was a young man, a small hunting party had fallen into the hands of the foreigners. The woman and her child escaped, but one man was tied to a tree and was shot. When he was 'a little bit rotten' he was boiled up and salt was added to the soup. The remaining captive was forced to eat his own brother while the foreigners laughed. He had escaped and made his way back to his people to report this horror.

At other times they had seen the strange growling beasts of the foreigners which were fed on the red blood of men. They knew when the men were being killed and their bodies emptied of blood because they could hear them screaming from inside their houses. It is not known to what the screaming refers, but the 'growling beasts' were generators, and the 'red blood' diesel fuel, which at that time was coloured red.

Stories such as these implemented the Wagrani's fear of cannibals, but Akawo still wanted to believe that Dayuma was behind these most remarkable gifts dropped from the skies.

The discussion was in full spate as some fishermen returned from the Curaray to report that some foreigners had come down in the wood-bee and were building a house on the beach right where one of the ancestors' trails crossed the river.

'Did you see Dayuma?' Akawo asked.

'She was not there.'

Akawo was disappointed, but not downhearted. It was decided that Gimari would go the next day with her aunt, Mintaka, to the beach and ask the foreigners for news of Dayuma. They also daringly decided that they would ask the foreigners to take them to her in the wood-bee. Some of the Wagrani were shocked at this proposal, but Akawo pointed out that the wood-bee had not hurt the foreigners. *They* had gone and returned in it many times. If it could carry them safely, it could carry a Wagrani.

The next morning Gimari and Mintaka left on their historic journey. Naenkiwi followed them. He wanted a chance to be alone with Gimari.

'We want to talk to you. Do not harm us. We are your friends,' Naenkiwi called out. The missionaries did not understand his pronunciation of the words they had so carefully learnt.

'Where is Dayuma?' Gimari asked.

The foreigners smiled and talked.

'Do you understand me? Where is my big sister, Dayuma?'

The foreigners did not seem to understand. They said many strange words which were like Wag, and yet were not. As the day progressed, some of the words became comprehensible, but were not understood in isolation. The Wagrani finally understood that the men were saying they were their friends, and these sentences were repeated over and over again.

'Dayuma, Dayuma, Dayuma,' Gimari repeated in her questions, but in the sea of unknown words, the one word that should have made sense to the Americans, was lost.

Gimari went over to the wood-bee. She rubbed herself against it and made flying motions with her hands.

'Take me to Dayuma, if she lives, in the wood-bee,' she bravely said.

The foreigners nodded and smiled. They gave her food, but made no attempt to take her to Dayuma.

Naenkiwi went to the wood-bee. He wanted to do something bold to please Gimari. He climbed into the plane. When the foreigners went, he would go with them. If he brought Dayuma back, or returned with news of her, or of any of the others who had gone to the outside, perhaps Akawo would think better of him. Not that it mattered what she thought of him; he would watch for his moment and he would kill Nampa and Gikita and take Gimari.

The men took him up in the wood-bee. It did not live, although it made a noise and flew. As a canoe sailed on the water, so it sailed through the sky. It was a remarkable discovery.

The view was also remarkable, so remarkable that since he could not grasp it, he dismissed it and looked at his people, who were astonished to see him.

They returned, but still the foreigners did not understand about Dayuma. It was nearly night; now was the time to take Gimari alone in the jungle, under the trees, away from her brother and uncle. Unfortunately for Naenkiwi's intentions, they met Gimari's family group on the trail to the river, setting out to see for themselves what had happened during the day, and hoping to be given some good axes. Naenkiwi was angry; he wanted Gimari alone.

'Go home,' he ordered them. 'The foreigners are not good. They tried to kill us. All day they were pleasant, but in the evening when it was time to eat, they tried to kill us.'

'What about Mintaki? Is she safe?'

'She is safe,' Naenkiwi said. 'She ran away and hid. Soon she will return.'

The disappointed party turned around and went back. Naenkiwi and Gimari slipped into the gathering shadows.

They returned to the houses later that night, and Gimari slid into her hut and curled up on her hammock. Naenkiwi returned to his own clearing to collect his machete and spears. His sister, Miñimo, guessed his intentions and followed him as he went to Akawo's house. He would kill Nampa and Gikita at once and then Gimari would be his. Miñimo started to scream as he neared the house, and at once there was a confused uproar. Naenkiwi was held and his spears broken.

Nampa pushed Gimari at her lover. 'Take her and go,' he said, guessing that their relationship had already been consummated.

'I won't let him have her,' Akawo screamed, pulling her daughter away.

The argument raged furiously, and finally the two lovers left together.

'Don't ever come back,' Akawo yelled after them.

When Mintaka returned in the morning, she was surprised at the chaos and anger.

'No,' she said, 'they didn't try to kill me. I didn't run away and hide. I sat there on the beach, close to their fire.'

'They would have killed you. They have probably killed Dayuma,' Akawo insisted.

'Naenkiwi lies,' Mintaka said.

By then everyone was spoiling for a fight. They were all disappointed at getting no information about Dayuma, and they convinced themselves that the foreigners were up to no good.

All the gifts were forgotten.

The row raged all day, and tempers grew to boiling point. On the third day after the foreigners had arrived, the whole group charged down the trail towards the Curaray while the wood-bee circled overhead before disappearing towards the beach.

Gimari was sent on ahead to stroll on to the beach and distract the foreigners while the men scattered to get into attacking positions. The plan was carried out, though there was a bad moment when the foreigners, realizing they were about to be attacked, produced their rifles, and fired over the heads of the Aucas to warn them off. When the Aucas saw that the foreigners were shooting into the air and not at them, they rallied, though one shot grazed Nampa's head as he hid behind the wood-bee.

The women darted forward to grapple with the foreigners and distract them while their men rushed up and speared them savagely at close quarters.

One or two of the missionaries were speared as they attempted to escape across the river. One actually reached the plane but returned to help the others. They speared him, too.

In their fury, the Indians ripped the plane to pieces, after removing everything of value for which they could find a use.

Within hours, the whole settlement was abandoned. All the presents of axes, machetes, and cooking pots that had been previously dropped to them were packed away in *chigras* and carried swiftly away down the trails.

Nampa packed the little chickens in a basket and took them with him.

Gimari and Naenkiwi thought only of the night to come.

10

After the Massacre – Rachel and Dayuma Go to the United States

RACHEL SAINT, AT SHELL MERA, remained in blissful ignorance of the massacre until the next morning.

The five wives, Marj Saint, Elisabeth Elliot, Marilou McCully, Olive Fleming, and Barbara Youderain, had no sleep that night as the air crackled with frantic radio signals. They did not know what to do. There was no message from the men. It was possible that their radio was damaged. If the women sent out a general SOS and the men were making headway with the Aucas, irreparable damage could be caused by rescue planes diving along the river.

Marj Saint informed Johnny Keenan, Nate Saint's fellow MAF pilot, that evening when Nate's plane failed to show up after dark. Night flying was prohibited over the jungle. Johnny Keenan took off for the Curaray at dawn.

Rachel Saint knew there was trouble when Johnny Keenan left so early: 'Nobody flew to that part of the jungle at that time of the day unless there was trouble.'

Then Rachel heard her sister-in-law, Marj, talking over the air to Betty Elliot. Marj said that the plane was smashed to bits.

'I just said "Aucas" to myself. Just like that. That's when I knew,' Rachel said.

When the fear, and afterwards the grief, abated, Rachel was furious.

Today she is diplomatic and says she was not angry, but Betty Elliot says otherwise.

'Rachel was heartbroken that she was not in on the secret,' Betty said:

It was not until a sandy beach suddenly formed on the Curaray in January 1956 that Ed McCully, Pete Fleming and Jim Elliot were able to make contact with the Aucas. Although they took rifles with them to 'Palm Beach' they made no attempt to use them in self-defence, and were speared to death rather than take another life.

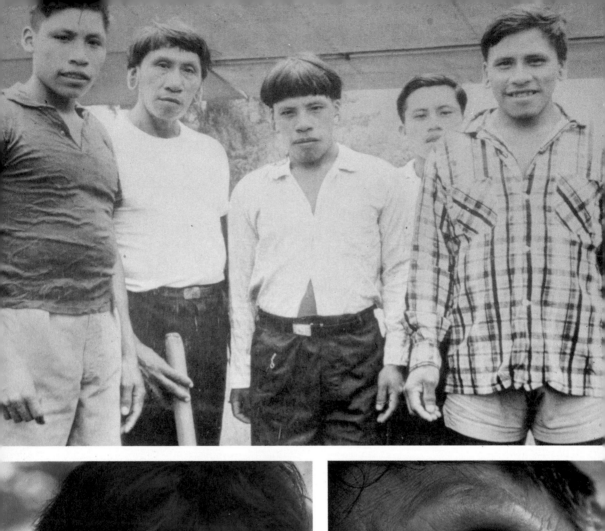

'There she was living right there in Shandia with us, and there was Jim flying in and out of the jungle all the time. He had even hiked up to Hacienda Ila to talk to Dayuma, and Rachel knew nothing at all about it.'

'Those fellows did what they thought was right,' said Rachel, 'and I have never criticized them for it. But if I had known, I could have helped with information, with language. I could have added my prayers. I just wanted to know.'

'She never really forgave us,' Betty Elliot said.

'I never understood why the men went in at that time,' Rachel said. 'I was making good headway with Dayuma and the language, and although I was sick at the time – quite ill in fact – I had every intention of returning to work with Dayuma. God had shown me how important the language barrier was. It was vital that we broke it first, before attempting to make direct contact with the Aucas.'

'The trouble with Rachel,' Betty Elliot said, 'is that she is probably the most stubborn woman in the world. She was very possessive over the Aucas, and was convinced that God had intended her to be the *only* one to work with the Aucas, and she resented any treading on her territory. If Jim and the others had asked for her help, she would have put in so many obstacles that it would have been impossible. They just had to do it their way. I and the other wives believe that God intended that sacrifice of the men in order to make the way clear for Rachel and myself to go in.'

The story of the Palm Beach massacre was published in nearly every newspaper in the world, and in *Life* magazine.

Overnight the bereaved wives found themselves famous. It was a notoriety they did not want, but the mission societies believed that many new recruits to the mission field, and many new converts to Christianity, would be won by publicizing the sacrifice the five young men had made.

As the only 'live Auca in captivity', Dayuma assumed a great deal of importance. Journalists, adventurers, and the curious were trekking into the Hacienda Ila to get her story, and many of them wanted to use her as a guide to go in and talk to the killers about their 'motives'. Most of the people were incredibly naïve, and had no real appreciation of what dangerous people the Aucas were.

Rachel laughed grimly when she was asked about the Aucas' motives. 'They have no motives,' she said.

She was determined to return as soon as possible to protect Dayuma from

Some time after Rachel Saint had begun to live among the Wagrani, this photo was taken of five former Wagrani warriors, including two (Gikita and Dyuwi, *second and third from left*) who were among the killers of 'Palm Beach'. BOTTOM LEFT: Dyuwi today – he still lives in Tiwaeno, BOTTOM RIGHT: Gikita (Dayuma's uncle) – the oldest surviving killer, who counts his victims in dozens. Today he lives in peace on the Curaray.

the 'scavengers'. She and her new partner, but old friend, Mary Sargent, walked from Shandia to the Hacienda Ila in March 1956. There had been no plane to take them in.

June 1957 to June 1958 was an astonishing year for Dayuma, and one she had no inkling would burst on her when Rachel reached the Hacienda Ila with Mary Sargent.

Dayuma ran to meet them. 'You came back,' she cried. 'I have shouted to the sky many times, Rachel, come back, and now you have.'

Dayuma was unaffected by the tragedy that was so recent and so important to Rachel. She knew that Rachel's favourite brother had died, killed by her own people, and she was sad because Rachel was sad. There were now many more strangers at the Hacienda Ila, and they all wanted to talk to her, Dayuma. She was nervous and had little to say. She understood what had happened; that five Americans had been killed on the Curaray. But what was so unusual about that? Her people were always killing.

Dayuma was only curious to know if any of the Americans had seen any of her own people, and if so, which ones. She longed to know if her mother, Akawo, her sister, Gimari, and her two brothers, Wawae and Nampa, still lived. This was the one thing no one could tell her. The jungle was like a closed wall beyond which lay a total mystery, before which lay tragedy.

A chink in the wall appeared when Dayuma looked at the photographs taken by the five men the first day they had landed on Palm Beach. She first saw the pictures published in *Life* magazine, and then she saw the prints Rachel had with her. Aunt Mintaka was recognized at once. She was a little doubtful about 'George', but thought she had seen him as a child. 'Delilah', she hoped, might be her sister Gimari, but since Gimari had been about eight chonta seasons old when Dayuma had left the jungle, it was hard to tell who the shapely girl might be.

Rachel showed her a colour photograph of all the gifts sent out by the Aucas. Dayuma brightened. She recognized them all, and could name, in Wagrani, every item, as well as all the different types of weaving.

Rachel took the deaths of her brother and his companions as the signal to work even harder with Dayuma. In a letter to her parents, Lawrence Saint and the former Katherine Proctor, Rachel described the five men lying in their unmarked graves in the jungle as being like 'five grains of wheat planted way down on the Curaray River in Auca soil', the harvest from which would be the Bible translated into the Auca tongue.

Lack of time was still the main problem. Despite the increased publicity and interest shown in the Aucas and in Dayuma, Dayuma's way of life was no different from what it had been. She woke before dawn, and was in the fields by first light. She slaved all day, and if Rachel Saint and Mary Sargent were lucky, she gave them an hour of her time after dinner at night.

Shortly after their arrival at the hacienda, Rachel and Mary found they were being roped in to help prepare for a major move. Don Carlos Sevilla was moving, lock, stock, and antique furniture, to another hacienda he intended creating in the wilderness. Don Carlos Sevilla liked challenges; once having got something good going, he would turn it over to a manager, and move on.

Everyone moved to the new hacienda, Hacienda San Carlos, some distance down the Anzu River. There Don Carlos started to build an airstrip almost at once. It was this strip that little Sam Padilla, Dayuma's son, spent many hours in trimming.

At the same time, Don Carlos Sevilla suddenly woke up to the fact that he had rather a famous Indian living and working as a common *peon* on his property. So Dayuma was promoted from field-hand to house-girl.

She was taken to Quito to shop, and her more usual Quichua garb of plain black skirt and smock-type blouse was replaced by a dress, decorated by patches front and back.

Rachel Saint and Mary Sargent now called Dayuma 'the patchwork girl from the Wizard of Oz', and they were in much closer contact with her during the day. She padded about the house in her bare feet, smiling with her wide mouth and big dark eyes. She was an extrovert, impish, alert. Mary Sargent wrote, 'We love her'. She also wrote of the other Auca girls who had come out of the jungle, 'The other three girls are with her. Looking at them, a strange realization wells up, almost as though it couldn't be; they belong to those others out there in that forbidden part of the jungle, over the ridge.'

Rachel worked with Dayuma for over a year, and between her prompting, and Dayuma's memory, they made good progress in the language, and with Mary's help, in analysing the grammar.

The first intimation of disruption in their routine came early in the spring of 1957. Rachel Saint heard on the radio from her director, Cameron Townsend in Quito, that Dayuma was needed for a television programme to be made in Ecuador on the life of Don Carlos Sevilla, who was known as the 'Daniel Boone of Ecuador'. Rachel was needed to act as interpreter on this programme, and so Don Carlos Sevilla agreed to release Dayuma for intensive language study for two hours a day. Rachel was very dubious about the programme, but was delighted with the extra time she could spend with Dayuma. She was not so pleased with the next message she received from Cameron Townsend in May.

The programme was to be made in America with the real Daniel Boone.

Rachel was requested to leave for California at once. She dug in her heels as only she could do so well. She told her publicity-conscious director what she thought of this scheme. Putting the average person under the bright lights of a television studio was bad enough, she said, but for Dayuma it would be a major shock. To combine that shock with taking her to Hollywood was unthinkable. There followed days of struggle, with Rachel praying, and Cameron Townsend making constant appeals. The public relations machine won, and Rachel, with Dayuma, was on her way to Hollywood.

'Rachel Saint – This Is Your Life' was screened before thirty million viewers on 5 June 1957.

Rachel herself went into a state of shock as she met her parents; her brothers; Beryl Walsh Adcock of Huntington Valley, her childhood home; Dr Addison Raws of the Keswick Colony of Mercy; Loretta Anderson from the Shapra tribe in Peru; Don Carlos Sevilla, and many others. The final shock was when Chief Tariri, the former head-hunter of Peru, walked into the studio. It was a collection of people that Rachel had not dreamed of seeing 'this side of heaven'.

At the Roosevelt Hotel in Hollywood that night, Tariri and Dayuma shared a big bowl of plain boiled rice and chicken, smuggled into their rooms. The artificial American food of spice-with-everything, and ketchup with that, was too much for them. Now that he was saved, Tariri was concerned for the soul of his 'little sister' from the jungle they both shared. Rachel found the whole situation too astonishing to grasp.

The next day, Dayuma was very ill, and this was to set the pattern for much of the year she was now to spend in the United States. For a girl brought up in the jungles of Ecuador, the number of alien 'bugs' in North America was a constant source of anxiety to Rachel Saint, but matters had been taken out of her hands, and at times she felt she was losing control of more than she cared to contemplate.

From California, Rachel Saint and Dayuma travelled to the University of Oklahoma, language base of the Summer Institute of Linguistics, for some intensive work in a language laboratory. Dayuma hated it. She was not used to sitting in a modern building, hour after hour, talking, listening to modern tape equipment, and talking again. She was frequently wandering off to help herself to Cokes from dispensing machines in the corridors.

Dayuma was in a cocoon caused by the language barrier, and Rachel Saint was her only means of communication. At times it was a very claustrophobic relationship, but there was not much Rachel could do, short of flying Dayuma back home to the jungle, and she was unable to do this since she had responsibilities to the people who financed her work in the first place.

New York, Madison Square Garden, and a Billy Graham revival meeting was next on the schedule.

'Think of all those folk out there as the turkeys you saw on a farm recently, and you'll feel better,' Rachel told Dayuma as they faced the vast live audience – a far more alarming experience than the bright lights of a television studio.

The sights of New York failed to move Dayuma, who had seen so much she could take in no more. The only thing that raised her interest was watching a window-cleaner in his cradle hanging from the Empire State building. 'How did he climb up there? Why doesn't he fall?' the jungle girl wanted to know.

Finally, Rachel Saint and Dayuma headed for Philadelphia, and home. Dayuma knew all about Rachel's mother. Katherine Proctor Saint had written constantly to her daughter at the Hacienda Ila. Rachel had translated and read aloud many portions of the letters that referred directly to Dayuma, and in Philadelphia the young Indian woman and Katherine Proctor, who was now seventy-six, had an instant *rapport* which deepened into genuine affection. Lawrence Saint had not long to live at this time, and Rachel was glad that she could spend so much time with him.

She recalled how, in her childhood, dancing, smoking, movies, gambling games of any type (including shove-ha'penny) were forbidden to all the Saint children, but none of this had been a sacrifice. On the contrary, Rachel was deeply satisfied that her whole life had been one of wholesome moderation, and for this she was grateful to both her parents who, she believed, had more foresight than most parents of young children.

Rachel and Dayuma were at that time quite famous. Everywhere they went, people would stop them and talk. While Rachel appreciated that they meant well, she found the interruptions and the fame distressing. She and Dayuma went to live in a quiet cabin in the Ozarks. Dayuma felt more at peace in the American hills, and their work continued with some of the pressures taken off.

During this period, Dayuma nearly died of a virulent type of Asian 'flu' that did kill many Americans. She took weeks to recover, and they stayed in the Ozarks far longer than Rachel had intended.

Astounding news reached Rachel on 18 November from her eldest brother, Sam, by long-distance telephone: some more Wagrani women had come out of the jungle. They had gone first to a Quichua village on the upper Curaray, and thence to Elisabeth Elliot at Shandia.

Rachel began to pack her bags at once, but Dayuma said she was too sick to travel. Instead, Rachel arranged for Betty Elliot to make tape recordings of the Auca women's conversation, and fly them to Dayuma.

Months passed as the tapes travelled to and fro between Dayuma and the Auca women, between the Ozarks and Ecuador. The net result, in solid information for Dayuma, was very little, but through the translations which Rachel made, Betty Elliot very quickly began to learn to speak Wagrani. She had a natural flair for languages which Rachel did not have. The result was that when Rachel and Dayuma returned to Ecuador at the end of May 1958, Elisabeth Elliot after six months' work, and Rachel Saint after three and a half years' work, were about level. One of the difficulties that Rachel had to face, but was then unaware of, was that although Dayuma remembered her tongue after some prompting, she did not remember it entirely accurately, and much of her pronunciation was at fault. Another problem was that one of the newcomers from the jungle had a speech impediment and could not pronounce her 'g's', and many months passed before all this was finally untangled.

Rachel and Dayuma left the Ozarks to go to Sulphur Springs, Oklahoma, where the climate was kinder to the Indian girl.

When Dayuma first saw snow falling in big soft flakes, she gasped and her eyes grew luminous with pleasure. She left her work in the kitchen to run out and enjoy it, but she was overcome by a strong desire for her eight-year-old son, Sam, to share her pleasure. She had not seen him for many months. He had been left on the Hacienda San Carlos with the old Záparo woman, and she missed him.

No one has ever quite explained why a Wagrani woman from Ecuador was lifted from the jungle east of the Andes and transported to America for nearly a year, where she became very ill, homesick, and missed her child.

Rachel Saint is not being criticized. She 'nearly went mad with frustration and anxiety'. It seems to be a case of those members of a congregation who are willing to support and finance a missionary wanting a little of the floor show, to make sure they are getting value for money. It is also a case of the back-room publicity boys of a missionary society having no real idea of the feelings of the missionaries they are publicizing. When Rachel was called 'a missionary super-star', many who support Wycliffe work were highly delighted. Rachel said she felt 'sick with disgust and shame' when she read the words. There must be a happy medium somewhere. Rachel Saint has said that the missionaries in the field spend more time writing reports for those back home than actually doing any work.

She did all she could to get Sam sent to America, working on this for months with no results. The biggest problem is that in a country where so much of the indigenous population is born unrecorded in the jungle, or high in the Andes, it becomes very difficult to obtain a passport.

Sam Padilla was born Ignacio Nobody. How to get records for him sufficiently trimmed in red tape to suit American immigration authorities was a problem finally solved by Captain Larry Montgomery of JAARS (Wycliffe's Jungle Aviation and Radio Service). He happened to be passing through Sulphur Springs to collect a Helio Courier donated by Kansas City to SIL for their work in the Ecuadorian jungle. Dayuma heard about him and made a personal request.

Larry Montgomery himself went to the Hacienda San Carlos looking for Sam. The next experience for the little boy who had travelled nowhere was in Captain Montgomery's plane, over the Andes into Quito. It was Sam's first plane ride and he was 'as sick as sick'.

Quito was no better. 'Can you imagine what it was like, to go to a town where cold winds blew off the high mountains? I was ice-cold.'

Worse was to come: a pair of shoes, his first ever: 'Captain Montgomery fitted me with a pair of regular leather shoes. They felt like a hundred pounds on each foot. I had to sit on the steps, then I tried to walk. I fell over. They felt ridiculous. The most heavy, ridiculous things in the world. So I sat on my tail and said I would travel like that.'

No doubt the citizens of Kansas City would have approved the first task of their Helio. Sam was in America, fully kitted out, within two weeks of Dayuma's request.

Sam remembers nothing else about his journey to Tulsa, Oklahoma, where Dayuma was waiting.

There was still snow. Dayuma had earnestly prayed that there would be some at the end of March when Sam arrived, and there was. As Rachel Saint put it, if the folk of Sulphur Springs wanted to know why there was snow so unusually late that year, they could consult with God, an Auca Indian girl, and her eight-year-old son.

11

Events Leading to Dayuma's Return to the Tribe

SAM LOOKED WITH INTEREST at the marigold in the Indian's nose. The Indian grinned and took the flower from a hole in his nostril and put it in a small hole at the top of his ear, fitted two overlapping feathers in the hole in his nose, and added other feathers to the lobes of his ears. His face was liberally daubed with scarlet achiote, and his lips stained purple.

'Nice, huh?'

Sam could understand him, even though he was a Cofan who lived north of the Napo and many miles from the Hacienda Ila where Sam had grown to be eight. He spoke Quichuan as his first language, Spanish as his second, and while he was in America, he had quickly learned to speak English. Quichuan is the indigenous language of Ecuador, spoken by a larger proportion of its native population than any other language. Most of the Indians speak their own local tongue, some Quichuan, and some Spanish, the official language.

The Cofan added an elaborate parrot-feather head-dress, similar in style to those worn by North American Indians.

He was ready to take Sam on a river trip.

Rachel Saint had taken Sam, of whom she was now very fond, to stay with some missionary friends at Lago Agria on the Cafanes River, and Sam was enjoying himself thoroughly, much happier there in the rich jungle than he had been in America. He had felt strange with his mother when he met her at Tulsa, having been apart from her for eight months. To begin with, she smelled different. In the jungle at the hacienda she smelled smoky and earthy. A good smell. She was barefooted.

Now he saw this smart woman who smelled of soap and laundered clothes. She had shoes and stockings, and a hat, and a thick woollen coat. She did not look more strange than Sam himself felt. His shoes were heavy, his long woollen socks itched and wrinkled and kept falling down. His hat with ear-flaps almost blocked all sound out, and he felt blinkered and threatened.

In time he grew used to the clothes, and to his mother's American smell. He did not think much of the toys of the boys he met, but enjoyed sledging, and all the ball games: 'I guess I was an active kid, not made for messing around with bits of plastic.'

Sam had been shown many things in America. Everyone had thought up new treats and schemes to entertain the small boy from the jungle, eager to see his amazed expression.

'I think I let them down,' he said. 'I just accepted everything as being part of life. When you're eight years old you don't analyse things too much. I think they all wanted to get a kick out of my kicks. I mean, there I was, a boy who had only seen a canoe. So they said, "Hey, Sammy, look at this great ship that sails over the great water." I think they expected me to faint with shock or something. My amazement would have made them feel good – the great civilized white man. Of course, I didn't feel that way then; I worked it out later. At that time I was just matter-of-fact. You have to have a concept of things before you can be astonished by them. But even so, I guess I was pretty confused inside.'

Events of great significance to Rachel Saint and Dayuma tended to slide over Sam's head. He just trotted along after his mother, or after Rachel, or wherever he was told to go. He had no idea when he returned to the jungle and to Limoncocha at the end of May 1958, that the two Indian women who arrived by air shortly after, pressing their noses against the windows of the plane almost before it had stopped rolling along the runway, were his aunts Mintaka and Maengamo from the Curaray.

He had no idea that in some of the taped messages sent to Dayuma in Sulphur Springs, they had described the continuing horrors of their land. They had told of Wawae's death, of the foreigners' deaths. They said that Akawo was 'living like a wild pig alone in the forest'. And they described a whole saga of bloody history.

News of Moipa's death had thrilled Dayuma; news of her brother Wawae's death had thrown her into despair; news of her mother had upset and confused her. She sent back taped questions to the two women living with Betty Elliot at Arajuno.

Their reply was typical of the Wagrani: 'Let her go and find out for herself if she wants to know.'

Now Dayuma was finally back in Limoncocha, anxious to find out. It was nearly twelve years since she had fled from the jungle, but her aunts recognized her at once through the windows of the plane in which they had arrived from Arajuno with Betty Elliot.

They were talking fast and volubly before the door opened, and they tumbled out, still talking as if to pack twelve years of history into ten minutes. Outside the plane, in the hot sun, they described again the death of Wawae, and told how his body had been dug up and hacked to pieces, so that the buzzards scattered his bones. Dayuma burst into floods of tears, but the women continued with their horrible saga.

That night, the three of them sat in a small shelter, alone, so that they could talk in private. Sam was with his mother on her hammock. He could understand very little, although Dayuma had been teaching him to speak the language of her birth. Rachel and Elisabeth Elliot sat at a distance, filling in details learned from the tapes.

Mintaka and Maengamo had left the jungle to look, yet again, for Dayuma. Her mother was still unusually obsessed with the idea of finding her daughter. She seemed driven by some force greater than herself to make contact with the daughter she had not seen for so long, even though she had other children, and even though she had disliked her.

'It's very strange,' Betty Elliot said; 'At one point Akawo was going to strangle Dayuma, and yet, she has searched so long for her.'

Mintaka and Maengamo and Gimari had arrived at the small Quichua settlement where Dayuma had gone to live with her husband, Manuel Padilla, but at the sight of habitation, Gimari had run like a deer back into the jungle. The other two were bolder. They made contact, and were taken to Elisabeth Elliot at Arajuno. The first tapes sent to Dayuma at Sulphur Springs had been recorded by Dr Wilfred Tidmarsh, an English missionary who was working at the Curaray settlement.

A few days later, some Aucas had hung around the Curaray settlement as if looking for Mintaka and Maengamo. They had finally killed a young Quichua worker, riddling his body with twenty-two spears, before vanishing into the jungle with his wife, Maruja.

Dayuma had been exceptionally upset by news of this event. Maruja's mother, Jacinta, had buried Dayuma's dead baby son by Miguel Padilla after the measles epidemic, and had cared for her. Maruja, as a child, had washed her and brought her fresh drinks and taken care of little Ignacio Padilla. Now she had been captured by Aucas.

When Dayuma discussed this with her aunts at Limoncocha, they were quite matter-of-fact about it. 'The men had come looking for us. They had lost a woman, so they took a woman. Why not?'

During the days that followed, Sam played with Elisabeth Elliot's blonde three-year-old daughter, Valerie, who followed him everywhere. He liked the child and was very gentle with her and looked after her well while all the women were talking together, hour after hour. Rachel had introduced Sam to the rather lovely, tall, blonde American woman, whose eyes were the same remarkable blue as her own.

'This is Betty Elliot who has been looking after your aunts from the jungle while your mom and you were with me in the States.'

'I didn't know what they were all talking about,' Sam said. 'I just knew that it was pretty sensational and important.' What was being discussed was Dayuma's return to the jungle to prepare the way for Rachel Saint and Elisabeth Elliot to go in.

'I am aware that Rachel wanted to go in alone,' Elisabeth Elliot said, 'and I can understand that. After all, she felt she had always been called and had worked towards that aim for years, while I was just an outsider. But the SIL insisted that Rachel was not to go alone.'

At that stage in late August, there was only the hope, not the certainty, that they could go. And at one point it looked as if everything would come to nothing.

Dayuma suddenly learned of her brother Nampa's death after injuries from an anaconda. The aunts described with great relish the wound in his head from one of the missionaries' rifles that had weakened him so that he could not fight the coils of the great snake. His lingering death had been horrible. 'He was cursed by the witch doctor,' Mintaka said darkly. (Later, Sam refuted these dramatic details, but the fact of Nampa's death was all too true.)

Dayuma felt that she could take no more. She had been looking forward to seeing her remaining brother. She grabbed Sam and left to walk to the Hacienda San Carlos. Almost immediately Maengamo screamed that she had been bitten by a scorpion, and Dayuma came running back.

A few days later, Rachel Saint, Elisabeth Elliot, Sam, Dayuma and her two aunts left for Arajuno, and from there, on 2 September, the three Wagrani women, with three puppies as gifts, set off on foot to walk to Wagrani territory.

Elisabeth Elliot remained at Arajuno, and Rachel Saint and Sam went to stay with the Cofans, where she tried to divert her mind by helping out in another mission field while she waited for news from Dayuma.

At the end of a month, Sam found Rachel distraught, her face white and tense. She held a collection of postcards delivered in the mail bag that day, and sent to her from friends in America. They all contained notes of condolence and regret that Dayuma had been killed in the jungle.

'Rachel was in quite a state,' Sam said wryly. 'She didn't know what to tell me. After all, it's not every day a kid learns the news of his mother's death on a postcard from the States. So she did what she always does when she's hung up over anything. She started to pray, and told me to do the same. I shut my eyes and there we were, praying away like mad. I had no idea what it was all about.'

12

Dayuma Finds Her Mother Again

DAYUMA WAS GOING HOME.

She retraced every step she had taken to the point where Don Carlos Sevilla had met her at the Oglán crossing with clothes. How long ago that seemed!

Then she had been a frightened, homesick Indian girl. Now she was grown up, with experiences she could not begin to describe to her people because they would not understand.

As soon as the Oglán was crossed, they were in Wagrani territory. The thick vegetation came right down to the river, and there was no trail cut to help guide foreigners into the secret places. Light and moisture came from the open river, and vegetation grew close to the ground, stretching out to the sun over the water. Here were thick thorn beds and nettles and prickly bushes to catch and tear Dayuma's frock. The women cut a wide path with their machetes; it did not matter, it would be overgrown again within a day or two.

Once the nearly impenetrable barrier near the river was passed, the forest trees soared to great heights, their slender trunks several yards apart, and at times travelling was easy. The women carried food for their journey, gifts from Limoncocha to their people, and the three fat puppies, so they were heavily laden, but they trotted at an easy pace, hour after hour.

Soon they found themselves back at the Oglán. They were lost. Only the men knew this part of the forest; they were the hunters, the raiders. The women knew no landmarks in the high country upriver, had no idea of direction under the heavy canopy of trees. They started once more, going more slowly, cutting a new trail and looking for signs of other trails leading down-river.

Dayuma was tired. It was not easy to get back into the old swing, the old smooth movement. Field-work had kept her muscles fit and she was strong, but the day had been tiring and the pace punishing for one who had forgotten it. She slept deeply that night in a palm-roofed shelter they quickly constructed, and started off again at first light. They had been two days on the trail.

The way was not easy now. They reached the headwaters of the Curaray where it tumbled between deep ravines, the rounded hills piling on top of each other, rising high on both sides. Small streams on clear beds of gravel and smooth rocks, grey, not weed-covered, cut across their track, running into the main stream. They climbed up almost perpendicular slopes to plunge down, balancing on roots to stop their headlong dive, never catching hold of the hanging vines – trees had thorns and vines had snakes. Dayuma followed her two aunts who never faltered, but balanced lightly and easily. She found she was now fitting into their rhythm.

They crossed from the Curaray to the Tiwaeno. The stream was smaller, more shallow, but more open. The water sparkled in the sun, the hills rose in a gentle blue-green haze of distant steam. The rounded stones and wide beach by the river was clean and innocent-looking. Dayuma found some large jaguar prints where the spotted cat, the biggest animal in the forest, had come to fish. But she felt no fear. This was her land. She still belonged.

The mist from the past was lifting. Over there was a sweet-potato patch. Beyond were wild bananas, small and sweet. Across there, her father Caento had built their house. She described all these things to her aunts, who had never lived in this part of the forest. They came from over the ridge separating the Tiwaeno from the Curaray, a day's march away. They decided that it would be safer if Dayuma stayed at Tiwaeno while Maengamo went to find Akawo. Akawo had said, 'Find Dayuma. Bring her back. If she has a child, bring him too. If she has no husband, tell her to come. She can hang her hammock with me. We will take care of her.'

Mintaka said, 'She will take care of you. She will find a husband for you and it will be as if you had never gone.'

Even so, Dayuma felt nervous. The spearing of Rachel Saint's brother was still very recent. Her people still killed.

The first night of their journey, Mintaka had told her of the fate of Naenkiwi who had taken Gimari from her intended husband, Dyuwi, which had caused all the trouble when the five missionaries came from the outside.

Naenkiwi had instigated an attack in the dark of the night on a group he thought were Downriver people in their hastily-constructed temporary shelters. He had been wrong. They were members of his own family returning from a downriver trip. He had speared his own brother-in-law, his own sisters' children. Many had died that night.

That had been bad enough, but now Naenkiwi had started to say that he would spear his new wife, Gimari, Dayuma's sister whom he had previously desired, but was now tired of.

After taking Gimari, he had taken Dyuwi's sister as yet another wife. The scores against him were mounting, and finally Dyuwi and Nimonga attacked his house and speared him. He was badly wounded and fled with two spears hanging from his body. Mortally injured, he returned to his house the next day. His family dug his grave and he climbed in, demanding that his infant children be thrown in with him, and one small girl was. She looked up at the sky with bewildered eyes as her father clutched her to him and the earth came tumbling in, thrown by willing hands. He demanded the other children, but they had been taken by their mothers who fled into the forest.

Gimari had taken her baby son, Dai. He would live, she said.

All this was told to Dayuma, who was now returning to it. It was not something that had happened in the distant past, but had taken place while she was in the Ozarks cabin with Rachel Saint just a few months earlier. In coming back, she was risking her life.

Dayuma did what Rachel Saint had taught her: she sat on a rock on the placid Tiwaeno beach and prayed for protection.

'Wagrani have always had a god,' Dayuma says today. 'My grandfather Karae told me about him, but we did not know who he was, or what the truth was about him. We did not know that we could talk to him, and that he was there to take care of us. Rachel told me, "a bird takes care of its young, and a jaguar its cub. God takes care of you. Why don't you then take care of your children and love each other?" That is what I tell my people. They have to stop killing and love God who loves them.'

The way to the Wagrani heaven was short and direct. After death, the soul – the spirit that was not seen but rushed through the air in the wind – went up along the trail towards their heaven. Lying across the trail was a huge worm, a grey jungle worm. The dead had to spear the worm and climb over its back to continue along the trail. A worm might not seem a very dangerous element, as a fiery dragon is, but it caused great shudders of revulsion in the minds of the people. The anaconda was their most feared enemy, and the worm fell into the same category. If it were not defeated and climbed over, if the dead could not face up to touching its body, could not face crawling over its great bulk, then they returned down the trail to earth as a termite, and as a termite they remained until they died. And that was that: oblivion.

Dayuma had been taught by Rachel Saint that Wagrani did not turn into termites if they failed to make the trail to heaven. They fell into the great fires that raged below the earth and lived, burning but not dying, in agony for ever. She wanted to tell this to her people, and to tell them that it was not fighting the worm that led them into heaven, but stopping all the bad things they were doing, like killing and taking many wives. Rachel had told her that God wanted this message to be told to her people, and that is why he would protect her. She waited calmly at Tiwaeno, secure in this knowledge.

When dusk fell on the second day after Maengamo had left, the puppies were rolling about on the beach, their bellies bulging with the fish Dayuma had speared for the evening meal.

Suddenly they stopped, their pointed tails stuck up and began to quiver, and they tumbled in fear behind Dayuma's legs.

She heard the familiar pounding thud of the Wagrani loping along the trail towards them. Her family were coming. She heard the once familiar yodels and answered with her own.

She had not used that unique Wagrani cry for many years, but it rang out loud and clear. The line of people broke out of the jungle, each vying with the other to be the first to see Dayuma. They carried no spears, only *chigras* filled with food. They were to have a feast.

Akawo was smaller than Dayuma remembered, and Dayuma taller than Akawo had imagined.

The night passed with talking and eating; there was much to tell. Akawo and the others had to repeat the news all over again; all the details that Mintaka and Maengamo had poured out in the days at Limoncocha. Then Dayuma had to tell her story, partly verified by Mintaka and Maengamo, who themselves had had quite an adventure while living with Elisabeth Elliot at Arajuno. She was able to convince them, finally, that the foreigners were not cannibals but lived well, and that they could live well with them.

Akawo shook her head. 'Some of them are devils,' she said, telling the story of the lone explorer who, completely lost and almost at the end of his tether, found himself in their territory only a few weeks ago. They could not kill him at once since he had a gun, and used it well. But they had followed him, and watched, and continually harassed him with their unseen presence so that he had no peace and was unable to sleep. On the fifth day he shot himself. 'Then we speared him,' Akawo said. 'But he was a devil, for when his body rotted, even the vultures would not eat him.'

Within a few days, the jungle had been cut back, and the former settlement of Dayuma's childhood rebuilt. Fifty members of her family had come, and during the following weeks, Dayuma told them about Rachel Saint, and the truth about God. They said they wanted to meet Rachel, and to hear the story themselves.

Dayuma explained that Rachel's name was Nimu – 'star' – after her own little sister who had been hacked to death by Moipa long ago.

Akawo was pleased. 'Bring Nimu,' she said. 'We will build a house for her and it will be ready when you return.'

When she had left Arajuno, Dayuma had arranged with Rachel that she would be away from one full moon to the next, twenty-seven days.

The moon was gone, and now it was returning and she had to leave or Rachel would come looking for her in an aeroplane, and she did not want to give her that trouble.

At the Cofans, Rachel was trying to establish the details of Dayuma's reported death. Where had her friends got that information? Before she could confirm that it had originated from a 'scoop' in the American press, based merely on Dayuma's disappearance into the jungle, Rachel received a radio message from Elisabeth Elliot at Arajuno: A group of Auca women and children were walking out of the jungle towards the house. Dayuma was in the lead, and she was singing 'Jesus loves me' at the top of her voice – in English.

'Sam,' Rachel said, 'your mother is back.'

13

The Start of Missionary Work
with the Wagrani in Tiwaeno

RACHEL SAINT, ELISABETH ELLIOT, DAYUMA and the other Wagrani
returned to Tiwaeno barely a week later, on 6 October. They took a large
party of Quichua porters to carry all they would need for many months, and
one of the porters carried three-year-old Valerie Elliot on his back.

They travelled for two days, as far as possible by river in dug-out canoes,
since neither Rachel Saint nor Elisabeth Elliot would be able to keep up the
punishing trot that was the Wagrani's usual method of travel. Even now, as
Rachel and Betty sat in the canoes, the Wagrani were loping along the banks
beside them, despite the fact that the canoes were moving down swiftly-
rushing highland streams.

They travelled down the Oglán to its junction with the Curaray, where
Dayuma had buried her husband, Miguel Padilla, and her baby son. Rachel
knew the story; now she saw the place.

The long views down the valley grew more wild and beautiful. Soon they
arrived at the junction of the 'Grape-tree River' – the Añangua, and the Curaray.
The Curaray continued its long journey to the interior of the Amazon, to Peru
and Brazil, but now they turned up the Grape-tree, making slow progress
against the rapids. Dayuma continued to point out landmarks from her tribe's
history: 'That is where the gold hunters came and were speared; that is where
Moipa speared the black man . . .' The details were always of death. Not
remarkably so, since what is there to report in the middle of a jungle where
one day succeeds the next in perpetual repetition of hunting, eating, living and
dying?

They were now in virgin territory. Animals came down to the river to drink. The trees were filled with birds and monkeys, and brilliant butterflies skimmed over the water. In time, this area was to be over-hunted by displaced Aucas as oil exploration, drilling, and new settlements moved into their land. But then, when Rachel Saint saw it, it was an unknown Eden.

They left the upper reaches of the Grape-tree and crossed the high ridge to the Tiwaeno; an exhausting trip for the two American women. As they headed down the home stretch, there before them was the new village, a collection of hastily-constructed palm-thatch huts in the newly-cleared jungle. Rachel said it was a 'sweet picture'. The welcome could not have been more friendly. She remarked in letters home that it was a thrill to see the copper-coloured bodies gleaming in the sun.

The bodies were not to gleam in the sun for long.

Wagrani who had gone out naked with Dayuma had returned with brand-new clothes, the gift of Dr Wilfred Tidmarsh. Rachel had plenty of clothes in the bundles carried by the Quichuas, and these were soon handed out before the Quichuas returned to Arajuno, something of heroes. Never before had any of them, except kidnapped women and children, slept in an Auca settlement and lived to describe the experience.

News of Rachel's arrival travelled quickly along the Curaray. Runners went to other groups, and runners from there went to yet further groups, and in a short time there were more than fifty Wagrani living around Rachel Saint and Betty Elliot on the Tiwaeno.

God's work could now begin.

Rachel wrote to her parents shortly after her arrival that the girls were charming and welcomed her as though they were 'débutantes from the White House'. She said Akawo, with her necklace and beads, was 'like a dowager'. This rather romantic image was not to remain long. Soon the 'scum of heathenism' was to be seen, and Rachel, whom Betty Elliot described as being remarkably naïve, was to see things that were an enormous cultural shock to her.

She saw a woman ignore and refuse to feed her dying husband, while his grave was scooped out under his hammock into which he would be tipped to save her the bother of hauling him into the bush.

'Why feed him and waste good food? He'll die soon enough.'

She saw men sharpening their spears ready to kill their daughters when a son died. The first time she saw this was when Tidonca openly cut hard chonta palm into long strips, then sharpened the edges and put barbed notches in. When Rachel asked him what he was doing, he said, 'Why should my worthless daughter live when my son dies?'

At noon, the boy died and Tidonca prepared his corpse for burial by doubling the boy's legs against his chest and tying them to the body with a vine. He placed a head-dress on the boy, and picked up his spear, looking at his daughter who was young and had no idea of the fate intended for her.

Rachel had not been able to prevent the boy's death. Until she could win the people's trust, it was better not to touch sick people, because if they then died, regardless of the reason, she would be blamed. But now that the boy was dead, she did the only thing she could; she grabbed the spear from Tidonca's hand and walked off with it.

'Nimu, leave me the spear,' Tidonca cried.

Rachel turned and held up one severe finger. 'No,' she said, 'you're not having it.'

Tidonca watched her, astonished at her cool nerve, as she turned her back and walked firmly away. Then he took his son and buried him. When he returned, Kimo, the man who had speared Nate Saint to death, was standing outside Rachel's hut on guard.

'She is my friend,' he told Tidonca. 'You'll have to spear me first.'

Rachel returned Tidonca's spear next day, a gesture of trust that meant a great deal, and made him her friend.

When Rachel was asked about the incident, she shrugged. 'If I'm to be hit by a spear,' she said, 'I'd rather have it in the back. I had no choice. If I had given in, that would have been the end of me. I didn't want any Wepes here.'

Wepe had taken over, in the Ridge area, where Moipa had left off. Whenever a really bad bout of killing began, Wepe was behind it. Rachel heard his name repeated constantly during her first years at Tiwaeno, and he became a great challenge to her prayers. The other great challenge was the sexual code of the group living on her doorstep.

'They were morally in the mud,' Rachel said, 'and it was a hard uphill struggle to make them see it. You can persuade men to stop spearing one another, it's not too much of a sacrifice on their part, and in the end, they can see the sense. But this was something else again. They had always been used to plundering women, and they couldn't see any sense in stopping. "How can it hurt?" they asked me, and I found it difficult to explain. But I saw that the entire hope for their future rested on Christian marriage. It is, in fact, their only hope, because it brings in emotion like true love, something they have never really known. It makes men responsible for their families, and once that happens, all the other good things follow.'

Rachel found it hard to sleep at night, knowing what was going on around her as the hot sky faded to black velvet and the stars fled before the moon. On such nights, even in the most civilized parts of the world, meek men are apt to bay at the moon. Somewhere in the village, a young blood would start to sing the Auca love chant, a message as old as time itself. He wanted a woman, and just about any woman would do.

A girl would slide from her hammock to obey that call; they were conditioned to do so, and Rachel would weep real tears of anguish. There is no such word as rape in the Wagrani language. When a man desired a woman, he took her there and then. And it was not enough for the girl merely to comply. She had to be proficient in the art of love. Her very life depended on it. Wagrani history is filled with the stories of young bucks who, rising from the hammock, have promptly speared the girl failing to come up to their expectations.

'I was shocked by what I saw,' Elisabeth Elliot said, 'but Rachel was more than shocked. She was heartbroken that such things existed in the world. I told her that she would have to take things easy for a while, not take them too much to heart. The fact that we were there at all was an enormous step into centuries of darkness. In time we could get round to handling the sexual habits. I thought there might be trouble if we spoilt all their fun too quickly.'

Elisabeth Elliot was probably remembering what she knew of the Jesuit missionary priest, Father Suarez, who had lost his life centuries earlier over that very issue. Differences of opinion over such matters came between Elisabeth Elliot and Rachel Saint, and after two years, Elisabeth Elliot left Tiwaeno.

'Rachel has a button-down mind,' she said. 'Both Rachel and I would say our standard was the Bible, but where we might differ would be on matters of interpretation – and a lot of things would, in analysis, be a matter of background and social prejudice.'

According to Elisabeth Elliot, the Bible does not frown on polygamy. She said she thought about this a lot when she lived with the Aucas, because when she started teaching them, she wanted to be sure it was what *God* said and not what *she* thought. In her opinion, God does not forbid polygamy and she was always arguing with other missionaries on this score. 'I said it was fine if they wanted to get up and give these Indians reasons from A to Z why it's economically and socially unwise to have more than one wife, but you can't say that God says they can't, because God doesn't say that.'

Elisabeth Elliot's opinion on this, of which Rachel Saint holds the opposite view, is that the primary evidence on which the Christian Church bases its teaching on monogamy is that God created one wife for Adam: 'which I don't think is a very strong argument, because after all, he did start with the minimum. He didn't create two men to start with; he only created one, and then he created one woman for him.'

In the New Testament one of the qualifications for bishops and elders is that they must be the husband of one wife, but Elisabeth Elliot says that it doesn't say anything about the rest of the Church. She interprets that as meaning that they must be the husband of at least one wife, which meant they should be married men. She agrees that there is a slight ambiguity here, although it is generally accepted to mean one wife as opposed to more than one – so when Rachel saw the number of wives the Aucas had, she pounced on them and tried to make them give up the custom. Elisabeth didn't see it in the same light; in the jungle, where man must hunt to live, it was necessary for men to take on widows and children, otherwise the women would die.

'This is one of the difficulties that Rachel and I had,' Elisabeth said. 'She was so positive about things and I would say, "Nobody could be more in earnest about obeying God than I – I want to do what God says and I don't want to do anything beyond that. If you can show me where polygamy is a sin in the Bible, I'll buy it." But Rachel can't – she can't possibly, but she's made up her mind and this was true of a great many things. All I could say to her was, "Well, you've got to live according to your conscience in the light of Scripture and I've got to live according to mine – and I am *not* going to tell an Auca Indian that God says he can't have two wives – or drink."'

This also was one of the issues between Rachel and Elisabeth, and perhaps a greater one than polygamy. The Aucas do not drink anything fermented – except *chicha*, and that is discarded before the fermentation is obvious – but when the question arose of whether wine should be drunk to celebrate Communion, Rachel took it as grounds for an absolute breach in fellowship between herself and Elisabeth. The trouble was that Elisabeth was not a teetotaller, and Rachel was, and according to Elisabeth Elliot, Rachel was not prepared to even discuss the matter. 'When we first discussed the possibility of having a Communion service among the Aucas she [Rachel] immediately took it for granted that I would insist on having wine in the service, and for this reason she told me she would never be able to have Communion with me there.'

Elisabeth told Rachel that she could use grape juice if she wished, although stressing that it was wine used in the Bible, but Rachel refused to discuss the subject. The very fact that Elisabeth had even contemplated the possibility of using wine was unthinkable to Rachel, and it was when the arguments grew more heated, Elisabeth left. She says that there were many more things that Rachel was stubborn over other than those of the Bible. Apparently one was that she wanted to keep the Auca tribe a pure one, and was 'furious when Dayuma kicked over the traces and married a Quichua' – as Komi is.

'Rachel is one hundred per cent dogmatic,' she said. 'I couldn't discuss anything rationally with her. She simply would not give way on anything. I haven't seen her since, although I have attempted to many times. She's just stubborn.'

Elisabeth Elliot is a woman of great charm and wit and elegance. Today she is a writer and lives in Boston. 'Rachel Saint is one of the most remarkable women I know,' she said. 'She won't give an inch on anything. But I admire her. I know what the Aucas were like. For her to have lived there amongst them for twenty years is nothing short of a miracle. She's entitled to her faults with an achievement like that on the credit side.'

Sam had not gone in to Tiwaeno with his mother. He was nearly nine years old when she left and Rachel decided that he should be educated, the first Auca boy ever to achieve that distinction. He was sent to a school in Quito financed by the Bible Missionary Society, one of the few Protestant schools in that largely Catholic town. He was put to lodge with a Quitan lady, Mrs Holenbick, who had two daughters, and two other pupils from the mountains.

'She had a hard job,' Sam said. 'I had to be taught to live and behave like a regular Ecuadorian Quitan. I had to be shown how to wear clothes. Sure, I had worn some clothes all along, and in the States, but I took most of them off at every opportunity. Now I had to wear them all the time and not rip them to bits. I had to eat with a fork – I had always used a spoon up till then – learn good table manners, good social manners. I could speak Spanish, but not all that well. I could not write or read it at all. I had to fit in. All I did for the first month was to cry for my mother and the jungle.'

There was not much time for tears. Sam was watched and checked every moment at home to 'civilize' him, and at school he was a long way behind. He went into the first grade and worked hard. His mother had told him to. He enjoyed school but was not a particularly good scholar. He was best at all sports, basketball, rugger, volleyball. In the sixth grade he was school captain of the basketball team. He also won a prize in art – a box of coloured pencils, 'not a bad prize in those days'. He was too ill to collect the prize at the official presentation (where photographers had been laid on to capture this great moment in Auca history). He collected it later from the President's office with a lot less ceremony.

Sam lived in Quito for six months, and then it was judged safe for him to go and see his mother. Rachel and Dayuma made the trip to Arajuno to collect him and take him in with them.

Akawo was busy in her hammock with a small bit of wild cotton and a simple spindle of wood when Sam arrived. She was making a *komi* belt for the grandchild she had never seen. The *komi* belt is a narrow cord of loosely twisted cotton thread that is worn by all Wagrani from birth. It is their only traditional dress. Akawo wanted Sam to be a real Wagrani.

As soon as she heard the distant yodel announcing their arrival, she hastily took a dress from the rafters of the hut and pulled it on, pulling it over her pot-bellied, sagging-breasted body. She was not yet forty, but had borne many children, and women age fast in the jungle. All her teeth were worn down to stubs. She looked at Sam's strong white teeth with admiration, and talked to him in Wag, although he understood little.

As Rachel predicted Sam, now living with his own people, learning to hunt, to use a blowpipe, to track, and to climb the highest trees, soon became proficient in the language. When the time came for him to return to school in Quito, he could speak it fluently. Akawo was not impressed with the names Sam or Ignacio, and gave him a new one. She called him Caento after her own father, and her husband.

This first visit to Tiwaeno was to set the pattern of Sam's life for many years, and he spent his time divided between school and the 'civilized' world, and a 'savage' life in the jungle.

In May 1961 it was considerably easier for Sam to go in and see his mother; the airstrip at Tiwaeno had been carved out of the jungle after a year of back-breaking work. The work had begun almost accidentally; a fishing trip had turned into a hunting trip, and many wild pig were speared along the river. Rachel used the great quantity of food as a means of getting all the men in one place at the same time to work on the airstrip. Gimari's small son, Dai, removed the first root from the location. It was his dead father, Naenkiwi, who had started all the trouble leading to the deaths of the missionaries at Palm Beach.

Rachel recalled how Nate had shown Naenkiwi how to make an airstrip with twigs and a model aeroplane, and now here was his son starting the 600-yard airstrip at Tiwaeno. Rachel recalls how very moved and humble she felt. 'God's ways are past finding out,' she said.

The next major event was the first Christian marriage, Wagrani style.

Dayuma married Komi, adopted son of Gikita, in August 1962. The wedding took place in the traditional way with a feast and dancing, and the couple were tied together in a hammock.

TOP: Three years after the massacre, Elisabeth Elliot and her three-year old daughter Valerie, Rachel Saint, a close relation of Dayuma's, Dayuma and Sam sit in the sun at Tiwaeno. BOTTOM LEFT: Sam, at Bible College in Florida. RIGHT: Rachel does her chores in Tiwaeno – where she remained, living mainly alone among the Wagrani for twenty years, destroying her health in the process.

A contrast between 'Aucas' in the Protectorate, where they wear clothes and have some modern tools, and 'Wagrani', two hundred miles into the Amazon jungle, who have had limited contact with outsiders. Sam lives freely with both groups.

Dayuma asked Don Smith, the first JAARS pilot to use the airstrip, to lead them in prayer at the end of the ceremony. The wedding cake was made by Rachel on the banks of the Tiwaeno, 'more miss than hit', as she put it.

A year later, Nancy 'Hummingbird' was born to Dayuma. The confinement on the hammock became complicated, however, and Dayuma was flown out to Limoncocha where the actual birth took place at the hospital there; the first Wagrani birth ever to be recorded in Ecuador.

There were many 'firsts' in those days, probably the most important being the registration of Auca land in February 1964. Dayuma was given the major task of selecting the area that was to be made a Protectorate, safe for all time against development. She drew up a plan for the Instituto Geografico Militar (IGM) which the government accepted. The land was called 'Dayuma's Auca Protectorate', and totalled 160,000 hectares, bounded by the Oglán River in the west, the Nushino in the north, and the Challua in the south – a one-hundred-and-fiftieth part of their former territory.

The fact that the Wagrani now had their own official parcel of land did not mean that they all lived there. There were several other major groups with whom Rachel Saint had no direct contact. There was the Downriver group who lived closest to the Napo, and raided on those borders. Then there was the Ridge group who, if anything, were even wilder. It was rumoured that beyond the Ridge there were even more Wagrani, a ghostly people with whom the Curaray Aucas had never had contact. Then Rachel heard of a small group known as Baiwa's Aucas living south of the Ridge people and the Curaray, and a small group of tearaways with odd habits known as the Splinter group, a band of young marauding killers with homosexual tendencies, made up of the wilder elements of all the other groups.

Rachel made astonishing progress with her own group, chiefly because of Dayuma's magical influence, but the task that faced her of taming the others was almost more than she cared to contemplate.

'The thing I had to remember,' she said, 'was that I was there to learn and record the language. That was my first priority. I had to learn the language and invent an alphabet and a grammar so that the language could be put into writing. My eventual aim was to teach the Aucas to read so that they could begin to educate themselves. I had to train teachers for the future.'

Her days were spent simply, listening to problems and offering advice like a village elder, and working on her translations. Some of the greatest difficulties in translation were the abstract concepts.

Catherine Peeke had gone to Tiwaeno as Rachel's language partner after Elisabeth Elliot had left. Catherine was working on her Ph.D. thesis in Wag at

Sam, the much-travelled young man who speaks four languages, with his
grandmother, Akawo, who has never gone beyond the jungle – and who has
seen practically all her family wiped out in spear attacks

that time, and her words probably best express the difficulties: 'There are deficiencies in vocabulary because Aucas have apparently lived without any cognizance of what the civilized world about them is doing. In this category lie the concepts of buying and selling, or even of trading; any form of specialized labour, as a carpenter, fisherman, teacher, sower; any religious or governmental organization, any concept of village or city; any idea of law, trial, authority. They know neither bread nor paper, so used their term for "wasp's nest" for both. "Wasp's nest food" is differentiated from "wasp's nest which is given-taken" (money) to which missionaries have introduced them. Coins are "fish scales" (metal is another unknown concept).

'They do not know horses, donkeys or cattle, and have never seen grapevines. (Rachel Saint named the Añangua, Grape-tree River.) They do not use grinding stones, nor know of stones used in building. Market places and political boundaries are unknown to them. They know no servant-master relationship. No rich, no poor. Teaching–learning situations are not recognized.'

The task before Rachel was a daunting one. She had to translate the Bible into a language which knew none of the usual biblical situations. How to tell the parable of the lost sheep, when they had never seen a sheep? How to say that Jesus rode on a donkey when they had never seen a donkey? How to describe a manger when they had no hay, no ox, shepherds or angels? How to describe the desert when they knew only the jungle? How to describe the Sea of Galilee when they knew only the river? The problems were endless. The completion of St Mark's Gospel at Easter 1965 was a milestone.

That summer, too, as a mark of faith, Nate Saint's children, Steve, Phil and Kathy, asked to be baptized at Palm Beach where their father had died. Rachel and Marj and the children were guided by the Aucas. Kimo, who, it was established, had actually speared Nate, led the group in prayer and performed the baptisms – the first Auca pastor – over the grave of the five men. 'Our tears, held back for years, flowed freely,' Rachel said of the Saints. Then, as she glanced up after prayer, she saw above the graves five red jungle flowers, 'standing straight and tall, with the sun filtering through that gorgeous forest!' It was an emotional moment, and they left the beach to its memories.

14

The Years Pass in Tiwaeno

'THINGS JUST SEEMED TO GALLOP ALONG,' Rachel said, when she and Kimo, her brother's killer, and Komi, Dayuma's husband, all went to Berlin in November 1966. She went first to her childhood home at Huntingdon Valley where her evangelist brother, Phil, was home on leave from Argentina. He had already met the two Aucas in the jungle when he had dropped in to see his sister, and he remarked how very different they looked in the depths of an American winter. They were wearing business suits, felt hats and boots. 'And what boots!' Phil said. 'They were enormous.' It had been a difficult job fitting their wide-splayed toes into normal American shoes. The three men grinned at each other, and there was a great deal of nodding and back-slapping, their only means of communication. Brisk and business-like, Rachel told Phil that she was off to the dentist, and that he was to give the Aucas a good bath. When Phil protested that he knew no words of their language, Rachel quoted, 'Ye olde monolingual method', and left him to it.

The two Aucas arrived in the bathroom in their hats and coats and were not too keen on taking a single garment off. While they were exclaiming over the 'wall of water' from the taps, Phil managed to remove their outer layers, but they refused to let their underlayers go, so he did his best with scrubbing brush and sweet-scented soap on the two half-dressed Indians.

Later, when he took them for a run to keep up their daily exercise without which they would have felt ill, the men insisted on running in single file, their perforated stretched earlobes dangling well below their crammed-down felt hats.

'If ever in my life I felt silly, it was then,' Phil said. 'I glanced at the houses along the way to see if people were watching. They were. I imagine the neighbours enjoyed our little procession as much as the Aucas enjoyed seeing the squirrels and the unfamiliar birds in the trees.'

Katherine Proctor Saint came to visit Rachel and her two Auca charges. She was old and wrinkled but stuck faithfully to a health food diet which gave her more energy than most eighty-four-year-olds. She had already met Dayuma, and was now delighted to see the men.

Rachel, Phil, and the Aucas watched a film shot in the jungle. Katherine Saint watched the Aucas. Each time one of them exclaimed at something familiar, she enjoyed their reaction and laughed with them.

That was the last time Rachel saw her. She died on 2 September 1969.

From Huntingdon Valley they went sightseeing in New York where, without doubt, the two 'wild men' were a sight for tame New Yorkers.

They were a sensation in Berlin at the World Congress on Evangelism. George Cowan, President of Wycliffe, wrote, 'The Aucas were terrific with their three-note melody, and their simple repetitive songs. During the closing hymn, an African delegate could contain himself no longer. He jumped up on to the platform and hugged each of the Auca men.'

A rapid tour of Wycliffe centres in Europe followed. It was the first time Rachel Saint had been to London since her 'vegetable dinner' when she was eighteen. It had been on that previous visit that she had the intimation of her future with an unknown people.

'I could not have known then, not even in my wildest dreams, that I would be back in London with two members of that tribe. At times, God gives me the most delightful rewards.'

The hall in Chicago, Detroit, Milwaukee, Minneapolis, Memphis, Kansas City, Dallas – it did not matter where, it happened the same way in twenty-seven cities – remained dark for a moment. 'Then a single spotlight flickered on, and there in the ray stood Rachel Saint in the flesh, a plump, grandmotherly woman, with greying hair stretched into a bun, piercing blue eyes and a face that fairly radiates. She spoke briefly, bringing the audience up to date on the latest happenings in the jungle. Then, with her certain flair for drama, she introduced the Aucas,' wrote Jerry Bledsoe for *Esquire* magazine in 1972. He met Rachel and the Aucas during their multi-media presentation on a gruelling tour of American cities. Rachel was not too keen on *Esquire*. She asked to see a copy before talking with Jerry Bledsoe.

'I told him it was better than I remembered it,' she said. 'It used to be the worst of the worst. Now it was the best of the worst.'

Rachel Saint had appeared on *This Is Your Life*, she had been on two Billy Graham crusades and had been to Berlin. Now she was on her own tour, a fund-raising enterprise organized by Wycliffe Associates, a group of Christian businessmen who used their specialized know-how to promote the work of the Wycliffe Bible Translators. This was the first missionary rally they had organized, and in Jerry Bledsoe's words, they needed a blockbuster to ensure their success.

And so it came to pass that Rachel Saint and her team were jetted out of the jungle and fitted out in smart new clothes.

Twenty-one-year-old Sam was the advance party. He went ahead of the team and appeared on practically every television network in the United States, and in every local newspaper. He was exhausted by the end of a week. It was his first time in the States since he was eight years old, 'And I saw nothing,' he said. 'Just highways, motels and hotels, studios and churches. I remember thinking at the time, what a strange idea my people would get of the outside. I used to look at all those roads, all those cars, all that concrete, and each time I would think, "This is what Gikita is looking at", or "What is Kimo making of that?" I can't imagine what they thought.' The men hated it, and Dawa vomited in the studios. They suffered the same nervous breakdown as Dayuma had suffered years previously, which was why she was not allowed to go again.

The rallies were a great success. People turned out in their thousands, and in several cities, two or three rallies had to be held to accommodate them.

Sam said, 'Never again. Once was enough for me. When you go to another country you want to see lots of different things. Every day was just interviews. I had two months just full with schedules, you know?'

Wycliffe had convinced Rachel that they needed the funds to help support their world-wide network in the field, but Rachel was not interested in funds. She did the tour, which was to be far more extensive than she had anticipated, because she hoped the example of 'saved' Aucas would help others to see the light which, in fact, it did. But during her absence from the jungle, a disaster occurred, and she was frantic with anxiety to get back to Tiwaeno to hear the details.

The first Auca missionary had been bashed in the back with an axe by Wepe.

Events had been leading up to that moment since 1964 when oil prospectors moved back into the Oriente. They looked at a new location to survey in the area around the Napo. Originally Shell had looked farther south near the Curaray. The northern strike was enormous. Twenty-seven companies were involved; Texaco-Gulf was the major company with an initial investment of three hundred million dollars.

The oil companies knew that Shell had previously been chased out by the Aucas, but by 1964 the price of oil was sky-high, and the Ecuadorian government needed the revenue. Nothing would stop them from going in now and there was talk of using guns, bombs, flame-throwers. Most of the talk was wild, but the result would be the same: a war between the oil men and the Aucas; a handful of naked savages standing squarely in the middle of fields of black gold, blocking the progress of the machine age. If it was to be a question of no oil or no Aucas, there was only one answer.

The oil companies looked to the government, the government looked to the military, and the military looked to Rachel Saint.

Work was speeded up to locate isolated Wagrani groups and to persuade them to settle in Tiwaeno. It was a marathon task, and few people took into account what was going to happen when several hundred Aucas arrived in a small area where there was insufficient game and few planted crops. The Aucas live by planting some distance from their settlement, and moving on to harvest them when they are ready, leaving newly-planted crops behind them. The jungle is full of *chacras* all in different stages of growth in the land that knows no seasons.

The oil companies surveyed and gridded the entire Oriente and areas were allocated to each company. Helicopter pads were established every three kilometres along the lines of the grids. Roads ripped through the jungle; long, brown, dusty tracks that by their very presence altered the ecology of the areas through which they passed. Airstrips were built. The government had an agricultural programme allocating fifty hectares of land free to each settler who had the courage to move in – and plenty came in from the cities – and the land was cleared in a burn and slash method. Towns sprang up. Coca, the town on the Napo originally called Porto Franciso de Orellana after the sixteenth-century Spaniard who explored the Amazon along this route, expanded dramatically with all the horrors of civilization that such a raw frontier town brings with it: venereal disease, pollution, television, and erratic, ugly breezeblock and tin-roofed shacks. There were no VD clinics. Quichuas spread the disease along the length of the river, and oil men brought it back into Quito.

The first step in contacting the still dangerous Wagrani groups was to devise a means whereby they could be spoken to without risking any lives. Nate Saint's loudspeaker from a circling plane had proved ineffective, so Don Smith, the JAARS pilot, constructed a small basket in which a transmitter was hidden under a false bottom, the antenna woven through the sides of the basket to conceal it, which was dropped by parachute to a Downriver clearing. Rachel, Dayuma, and a Tiwaeno relative of one of the main Downriver group sat in the circling plane and held a direct conversation with the Wagrani below, and after bargaining for an axe, they agreed to travel to Tiwaeno. Their relatives from Tiwaeno set off to meet them and to guide them in.

Unfortunately the meetings were hampered by a series of delays and accidents; one woman was bitten by a snake and had to be carried; others changed their minds and returned to the Downriver settlement; sometimes the guides and their Downriver relatives lost each other. Eventually, however, the Downriver Aucas arrived. First a group of one hundred and four. Then fifty-six. Rachel Saint realized that the heathens outnumbered the Christians in the overcrowded, noisy village. 'What we had,' she said, 'was a head-on collision between a Christian community and a totally heathen community. And it was some collision. Things haven't been the same since.'

The Downriver group viewed their relatives with suspicion and distrust. They had not expected to see a white woman who had 'rain in her eyes'. The school had to be closed down because the girls could not walk home at three o'clock in the afternoon.

'The Downriver men's morals were rotten, minus,' Rachel said. 'Boy, I tell you, this crowd . . . scum. We even had to close the night school we had for adults because nobody dared be out after dark for fear of being speared.'

There were increasing incidents. Food was stolen, girls were taken into the bushes and the 'illegitimate' birth rate spiralled. Converted girls were frightened of Rachel's reaction when they produced their babies, so there were attempts to drown them. Rachel had a difficult job in checking up on who was giving birth, and making sure that the child was produced alive.

One converted young woman committed suicide when she discovered she was pregnant. Sam said he was puzzled by the dead girl's motives. 'I didn't see why sitting in a hammock and tying the knot made all that difference to having a kid. She was having a kid. Fine. Someone would look after it. Everyone brings everyone's baby up in the tribe. I didn't see why she had to go around taking barbasco fish poison.'

Worse was to come.

Polio arrived and spread through the tribe like wildfire. The first to die was Amoncawa. They thought he had 'flu', and left antibiotics, but were concerned when he started uncharacteristic frothing at the mouth. After his death, his half-brother Iniwa grew very angry. He said that Piyamo, a witch doctor from the Downriver group, had put a curse on Amoncawa. Iniwa was one of Sam's childhood friends who had gone with Sam on all his fishing and hunting trips during his school holidays from Quito. He had been baptized at Palm Beach, along with Nate Saint's children. Sam said he was an example of how most Wagrani are basically the same underneath. 'Religion and so on, that's superficial with them. They are their ancestors' people and under stress, it shows.'

Sam was bathing off the beach at the Curaray settlement with Iniwa and some other young men. They were discussing Amoncawa's death. Iniwa suddenly jumped out of the water. 'Hey, you fellows,' he shouted, 'I'm going to get this witch doctor. Let's go.'

They thought he was joking until he put machetes and a big knife in his canoe.

'Despite being with Rachel all these years, he was still himself,' Sam said. 'I couldn't imagine that he would actually do it. Two of the other kids went with him, but I wasn't going to lose any sleep. It was their decision. They have their freedom to make their own mistakes.'

The three youths made their way to Piyamo's son's house. They decided they would kill him first so that he could not come after them when they had killed his father. They waited until the early hours of the morning; Wagrani have an almost telepathic sense when someone else is near. They feel the air move, and they smell them. Near dawn, when they are deepest in sleep, is the traditional time for killing. Everyone was sleeping, not worried about an attack, as there had not been one for twelve years in the Protectorate.

When the three men located their victim, the hut was immediately in an uproar. They tried to pacify all the other occupants by telling them not to fear – they were not after them. In the confusion, Piyamo's son escaped into the bushes, and spears were thrown at him as he went. He was badly injured in the liver, and died two days later.

Meanwhile the three young men went looking for Piyamo, but he was away hunting. By the time they returned to the Curaray, their victim had died, and the news was all over the river. Dayuma, who was harvesting crops on the Curaray, radioed Rachel at Tiwaeno.

Sam met his young friends on their return.

He said: 'Hey, you guys, you've really blown it now.'

They said, 'Why? We've been spearing pigs. We didn't get them all so we're going to have a sleep and then we're going back again.'

Sam said, 'I looked at them and saw that their faces, their whole expressions, were completely different. It's true what they say about when you kill a man. Something in you does change. These guys had gone back to being Auca – wild.'

Sam decided to go fishing, a walk about two hours away. The other young men said they would go with him. When they returned in the evening, laden with fish, Iniwa suddenly went rigid, gazed fixedly into the air and said, 'Oh my God, what is this?' Something seemed to hit him. His friends were amazed. He threw himself down on the sandy beach and started writhing around. Sam thought he was joking. Then, as quickly as the attack had occurred, he was himself again. He dusted himself down, and said, 'Okay fellows, I'm fine.' He bent to pick up the basket of fish. Then the same thing happened again. This time he started to shake and completely lost control of every nerve. From his feet to his head he vibrated. He seemed to be blind and deaf. Then his vibrations slowed down. 'Slower and slower like a spinning top,' Sam said. 'It was creepy. We all stood about watching.'

Iniwa then keeled over, and was found to be rigid and dead. 'It really frightened the other two who had speared Piyamo's son,' Sam said. 'They kept watching each other to see signs of the same curse.'

Sam, personally, has no idea what caused Iniwa's death. Many others were dying of polio, but the doctors said that that was not the cause of Iniwa's death.

Rachel Saint has no doubt at all about what killed him. 'It was the judgement of God,' she said.

The relatives of the Downriver group were sharpening their spears to launch a retaliatory attack. Rachel, alarmed, went from man to man telling them to put down their spears, and does not know what would have happened if the polio had not struck nearly every member of the tribe.

As people started dying, and sixteen died altogether, their relatives grew more frustrated.

'They'd bash in everything that belonged to the person, and burn the house down, and furiously rant around and, in the case of the men, pick up their spears to kill,' Rachel said. 'It was impossible to bring in a doctor to diagnose what was wrong. He would have been speared instantly. People were dying all around. Nobody was even well enough to bury them. All the old Auca ways came to the surface. It was worse with the Downriver group there – we hadn't had a chance to get to work on them. When parents died, the kids were being chucked into the graves. I'd be running all over, grabbing the kids, and saying, "No you don't. Not these kids. I'm having them." Then I would put them in my hammock in my house, stick a banana in each of their hands while I had to run off and rescue someone else. It was all hell let loose.'

Rachel herself went down with the disease, and for days was too weak to move. She propped herself up by the radio, and Dayuma carried the full brunt of nursing the sick.

Doctors and nurses could come in force only when all the potential killers were too ill to move.

In due course, when the sickness passed and the dead were buried, sixteen Wagrani were left crippled, and an unimagined sight was seen; wheelchairs in the jungle.

Sam is very angry over the whole episode. He is convinced that the virus was carried in by mission contact. The missionaries have always stuck to the story that it was carried by a group of Quichuas travelling downriver to fish.

'It was one of the saddest things the tribe went through,' Sam said, talking of the epidemic. He maintains that it has nothing to do with the jungle, that it is a North American disease. 'Why did they have to blame the Quichuas? Why don't they have the nerve or courage to admit their own faults? Blaming the Quichuas, so far as I am concerned, blew the whole thing. If the Quichuas had polio, we would have seen it. Not one Quichua went down with polio, and that should tell people a lot.'

Sam thinks it is time the truth was told about many things, and he has made himself the person to do that. He claims that his uncle Nampa, Dayuma's brother, was not killed by a boa, or by a witch doctor as the missionaries claim, but solely by the .22 bullet from Nate Saint's gun that lodged in his skull.

'When Nampa came back from the killing on Palm Beach, he had a real bad pain in his head. Really weird. It nearly drove him out of his mind. He died after two weeks. Now, the whole tribe tells me this. Everyone who was there saw it. Okay, he had helped to spear the missionaries, which is bad. He deserved a bullet in his head. So why do the missionaries pretend otherwise and write all that stuff about boas and curses?' Sam explained that none of the people in the tribe have any idea what has been written about them because they have no concept of books.

'Apart from Rachel, and maybe one or two others, I am the only person in the whole world who can put over the Wagrani point of view. The missionaries can say this is so, or this is what is said, and no one would know the difference. Except for me. I want to bring all the truths and the facts out, so my people can have a say. Now the missionaries say I have the Devil in me. Maybe, maybe not. But people look up to missionaries, and some of them are good, and some of them are bad. People have to know these things. They have a lot of power over people's lives.'

After the polio epidemic, pressure was brought to bear on the SIL to attempt a breakthrough with the Ridge group, Wepe's people. Oil company exploration was within a few miles of the Ridge, and a worker had been speared to death. The ideal person to go was Toña, an intelligent young man who had been taught to read by Rachel Saint, and was learning to speak Spanish. He was to be the new teacher in the bi-lingual school planned for the future. Wepe was Toña's half brother, and at Tiwaeno they all thought that he could get through to him if anyone could. Preliminary air-to-ground conversations were attempted, and eventually Toña decided the time was right to go to the Ridge.

For a year, there were radio messages from him. The first ones made sense but the latter ones were confused. News finally came through that Toña was dead.

When Rachel returned to Tiwaeno from her American tour, she pieced together an incredible hoax on the part of Wepe and the Ridge Aucas.

Toña had been killed within a few weeks of his arrival, hacked in the back with an axe. Thereafter, his nephew, Kiwa, had impersonated him on the radio. The messages were taped at Tiwaeno and sounded odd, but authentic.

Eventually, arrangements were made for 'Toña' to return.

In Rachel's absence, Catherine Peeke went in an oil company helicopter to pick up Toña and Wepe. She was introduced to Toña, and looked at him in astonishment. This was not Toña – and yet, Wepe said he was, and he himself said he was. She pretended to agree, and the unsuspecting pilot delivered potential dynamite to Tiwaeno, where there was safety in numbers, and Wato, Toña's wife, immediately exposed the imposter.

'You are not my husband,' she said.

Kiwa insisted that he was. Photographs were produced to prove that he was not. He was asked to read and write. They asked to see under bandages tied round his leg where Toña had a bad crocodile wound. He declared that the bandage hid an axe wound, and fell to the ground, writhing in simulated pain.

Wepe suddenly took to his heels and ran towards the jungle. The others fetched him back and intended to spear him but were persuaded not to. Wepe was shown a map of the jungle and they interpreted it for him. When he saw the Ridge and the network of oil trails surrounding his home indicating the closeness of civilization, he fainted. When he came round, he asked to be returned to the Ridge. His son, Kiwa, remained.

15

Sam Goes to College in the United States

SAM WANTED TO GO TO COLLEGE. He liked the idea of living in the States, eating hamburgers, drinking Coke, dating neat blondes, and altogether being a regular campus guy. He did what he always did in those days: he went to see Rachel to talk it over with her. Rachel was pleased. 'Well, Sammy,' she said, 'You know this is what I have always hoped for.'

She said she would talk to her director at Limoncocha, Don Johnson, and see what could be done.

Sam took a job working with the French oil exploration company, Geophysical, as an interpreter and guide. The pay was very good, three hundred dollars every three weeks, and all expenses paid. Every fourth week was an unpaid holiday. He saved hard towards his college expenses, and waited. Eventually the message came through. It was all fixed. He was to go to the Memphis Baptist College.

One of the girls at the SIL telephoned him, 'This is fantastic, Sammy. We always hoped that you would one day take over Rachel's work when she leaves.'

Sam realized then that the Memphis Baptist College was a Bible School. He was philosophical. 'I figured that it would still be okay. I had an image in my head about college in the States; young kids, lots of fun, some work.' What Sam did object to was the feeling that he was being pushed into a situation not of his own making. He felt that too many assumptions were being taken about his future.

He resigned his lucrative job and waited for a place to be assigned to him.

He waited for five months, during which time his savings were reduced. Finally word came and he arrived at Memphis, Tennessee, in January 1972. The President of the College met him in person at the airport and took him to lodgings with the pastor of a local Methodist church.

Sam felt his spirits drop when he enrolled in class. Instead of the busy campus filled with students in jeans, he saw 'quite a few elderly folk. Women weren't allowed to wear pants. I don't think there were more than fifty students in the whole place.'

The pastor with whom he lodged was remarkably strict with his own son, and treated Sam in the same way. Sam could understand that to some extent, even though he was then nearly twenty-two. He decided that since he went to church every day, at school, he would take Sundays off to be with his girl-friend, his first American one.

The pastor ordered him to church. So Sam left and found lodgings of his own with a widow who fed him well, laundered his clothes, and generally mothered him, all for ten dollars a week. Life was more bearable, but when Rachel phoned him in April from Tampa, Florida, where she was at a conference, Sam told her he felt 'Terrible. Miserable.' He explained that he found the Bible School so unenlivening that this had influenced his attitude to the whole town, which was, in fact, a beautiful place. 'I hated it. I couldn't wait to leave.'

Sam flew to Florida to talk to Rachel. He was as pleased to see her as if she had been his mother. He liked Florida immediately. The climate suited him, and after the tension of Memphis, he slowly unwound.

'I'm always having battles with Rachel,' Sam said, 'But I'm always very glad to see her. She's like my mother. I love her in that way.'

Rachel did her best for him now. She found him a place in the Florida Bible College, and paid his fees.

The College was more like an hotel. In fact, it had been a luxury hotel, bought up with all its fixtures and fittings by Dr Ray Stanford. It was a huge old building with two tennis courts in the flower-stocked grounds. There was an Olympic-size pool where Sam shone, and a lecture room where he did not. Off the entrance hall were beauty parlours, coffee shops, boutiques, magazine stands.

The sleeping quarters had not been altered since they had been bed-and-bathroom suites for paying guests.

'It was quite a fancy school,' Sam said. 'It was still a religious school, but more liberated. I thought I would do all right.'

Dr Stanford welcomed him warmly as the son of Dayuma. He felt like a

Hollywood celebrity. 'I had no idea so many people knew my mother.'

Sam decided to create a good impression. Most people registered for the minimum of nine hours' lectures a week. Sam registered for eighteen.

'Everyone asked me, and when I said "eighteen hours" they all said "Wow!" I felt very good. I wanted to do well there.'

Since Sam had booked for so many lectures, he felt that he could afford to cut a few that he did not like. At the end of the third week he discovered that the classes he attended were down to four. He increased the number of classes, but not the hours. Attendances were checked by a fifteen-minute test at every lecture. He went to the first lecture each morning, regardless of subject, took the test from his seat right at the back, turned in the paper, and headed straight out of the door. He would return to bed and catch up on his sleep, or take some books and go to the beach.

'I was supposed to be studying the word of God. I found that I was studying instead the works of God.'

He found American girls, especially those who sunned themselves on Miami's beaches, fascinating. He liked their Americanness, their wholesomeness, and their frankness.

No one had ever suggested marrying him off in Tiwaeno, and when he was asked if he had ever considered marrying one of his own tribe, he was cautious. 'I've thought about it, sure. I had no one in mind. I was friendly with all the girls, but I never had a "girl-friend" in the jungle. That's not the custom. I don't think I could marry a Wagrani girl, though. We wouldn't have a great deal to talk about.'

Life was not all play. Sam had to work for his bed and board, though not for his school fees, which Rachel Saint paid. Students who had limited means worked for the school for a few hours each day. They gardened, cleaned the rooms, or served at table, for which they got a fifty-dollar voucher which could be written off against food eaten in the restaurant, or clothes bought in the boutique. Extra work brought an extra ten dollars' spending money. 'For me it wasn't too exciting working as a cleaner. I preferred to make money by using my head,' he said.

He soon found the means through two old friends, Tom Adams and Dave Armstrong, whom he had first met in Quito on holiday. He never quite understood why they were at Bible school. They were young men of private means who cut most classes and finally rented a large house near the beach with its own pool. They also ran a sounds system business which they set up shortly after meeting Sam, and they asked him to join them. Sam gave up his domestic chores at the school.

Emancipation came for Sam in the shape of a five-hundred-dollar cheque from the Quitan lady, Mrs Holenbick, with whom he had boarded as a school-boy. With the cheque was a note: 'You are like a member of my family, and I am very proud that you are at College. I hope this will help you out in your studies.'

Sam had no intention of investing in his studies. He wanted to invest in some fun. He bought a motor bike.

That summer, Sam and his two friends took over the town and the beaches. Sam was earning money, dating girls, having his photograph appear in the local Miami papers and, every so often, in the local celebrity pages, and was living out his American teenage dream.

The President of the school, Dr Stanford, called him into his office. Sam was not insured to ride a motor bike, he said. Sam protested that the bike was insured, but though all college students were insured against medical expenses, this did not include motor-cycle accidents. If Sam had an accident, Rachel Saint could not be expected to foot the bill for any hospital fees. Sam saw the point and promised not to ride the bike. Within twenty-four hours he was zooming towards the beaches on it. 'I was hooked on that machine too much.'

The third time Sam was warned, things began to look serious, so he sold the motor bike to be better able to resist temptation.

With three years of college behind him, qualifying him for nothing he wanted to do, Sam returned to Quito and took a job as a guide on the flotel *Orellana*, moored at Coca. It was a large flat-bottomed floating hotel, as the name implied. Tourists were flown in over the Andes from Quito, in itself a sensational experience, then they travelled down the Rio Napo, taking canoe trips and hikes along jungle trails during the day.

Sam was a very good and popular guide. He still gets letters from all over the world from people he escorted along the trail. It is not often a guide belongs to one of the most dangerous people in the world, is skilled in woodcraft, is witty and attractive, and speaks so many languages. Part of his duties included slide-shows and lectures. Sam was adept at this and showed many of his own slides.

He frequently met the Wycliffe staff at Limoncocha, where flotel passengers stopped for a lecture on work among the Indians, and to visit the local artefacts store.

Sam was welcomed at Limoncocha until the report of an interview with him appeared in the Quitan newspapers in which he had made some unflattering remarks about the work the missionaries were doing in the jungle.

The only 'missionary plus', as Sam sees it, is that they have stopped his people killing each other, which *is* a very big plus. But Sam can see a future where his people will be absorbed and integrated into the general mill of 'Quichuan' Indian – belonging nowhere and having nothing.

'The Oriente is their land. They are entitled to live in it in their way for all time. Sure, I understand about oil. Well, let the people take the oil; we don't want it. We want our freedom. Missionaries just don't understand about freedom. Certainly not in religion.'

Sam maintains that he believes in God, but not in religion, which is man-made. He has studied the subject thoroughly and understands the difference between belief and dogma. The missionaries, he says, have no respect for other beliefs. 'I respect what anyone wants to believe or say. That's up to them. But the missionaries respect nothing. They force their ways on everyone, just because those people are too frightened or ignorant to know how to fight against them. The only way my people knew was to kill, but if we had not defended ourselves in the past against the invaders, where would we be to-day? Taken over and wiped out – like the Záparo – like the Inca.'

16

Sam in Quito Today

SAM MET CHRISTINA BONNICK at a Fourth of July garden party given by the United States Embassy in Quito.

'I looked across and there was this face, oh, just shining out from all the rest. I knew I had to have that man,' Christina said.

'I was there to hustle the ladies,' Sam said.

Christina had walked over to the bench where Sam was sitting. She said nothing, neither did he. He looked at her, then patted the seat next to him.

'I've been saving it for you,' he said.

'So cool, so arrogant,' Christina said. 'I didn't even know what language he spoke. I thought he was a North American Indian, an Apache, or something. I could do two things. I could go, or stay.'

She stayed.

Christina said, 'After about fifteen minutes, I had got what I had gone for.'

'She really had her hooks into me,' Sam said.

She gave him her phone number and asked him to phone her at six-thirty that evening. It was then four-thirty. He called her at exactly six-thirty. They went to a party where they danced all night.

'I was so positive,' Christina said. 'I knew I wanted him.'

He called on her the following afternoon in an enormous American hired car, and left the engine running.

'It was neat the way he did it. "I've left the gas tap on at my place, and the water pipes have burst. There's going to be an almighty explosion. Let's go".'

'I gave you the choice,' Sam said. 'You could have come with me, or you could have stayed.'

'Some choice. You knew what I would do.'

'We went back to my place. Boy, that seduction scene!'

'It was so unsubtle.'

'You were star-gazing,' Sam said. 'Star-gazing in the middle of Quito. You asked me to look at those stars, and then you grabbed me.'

'I knew I wanted you, so I did what I'd never done before. I seduced you. Waking up was lovely, lovely, lovely. There I was . . .'

'And there I was, looking at this blonde girl right next to me trying to figure out what had happened.'

They had breakfast out. And lunch and dinner. Sam had to order every meal. Christina could not concentrate on the menu. When the food arrived, she did not eat it.

'I couldn't even think about eating. He was so beautiful. And there was this great plateful of meat. I was practically a vegetarian then.'

They drove out every day for all their meals. They spent six months close together. Every minute for six months. Christina could not understand Sam.

'There was this wonderful guy. He didn't work. I didn't know what to think. I thought he might have inherited money. He said nothing, absolutely nothing, about himself. He just left me to guess.'

Then Sam ran out of money and he had to get some more work as a guide and translator. This was easy, as no one else had his unique combination of talents. He moved into Christina's small garden apartment with its hanging vines and humming-birds' nests, and Christina learned a great deal more about him.

'But not all. He's very silent about himself. He tells me things, really important things, at the very last moment. I never know what to expect.'

Christina is tall. Her legs are long and slim, and she wore tight, patched blue jeans, no bra, and an off-the-shoulder blue cheesecloth smock. Her eyes are round and thick-lashed, the blue of an English spring sky. Her blonde hair was in a smooth curved bob – 'I got it cut for my TV show'. She is English and teaches yoga. She went to Quito by accident in 1974 and has been there ever since.

'South America is like that,' she says. 'It's a very strange country. It takes hold of you and you allow it to happen.'

Quito is a cosmopolitan town, full of people from all over the world who have come, many by chance, and stayed. It is a wide-open, exploding town, with oil and expectations pouring out money and opportunities in unrefined abundance. One day, perhaps, it will be tapped and controlled. Now it has the urgency, the excitement of the Wild West of a hundred years ago.

Sam describes his country as the start of the New World. 'It's been called that for five hundred years, and it's still new. It's all that's left of richness and wildness, and it's got to be kept that way. The rest of the world is washed up, overcrowded. We can't let that happen here.'

Sam's strong feelings about his country are accentuated, in a way, by his dual citizenship. He is of the High Sierra Central Valley of the high Andes where Quito is situated, and of the wild land beyond: the land of the Wagrani. In his own mind they are divided, but are both his, and he feels that the wilder land needs more consideration and protection. Quito and the Andes will always be there, but once the Amazon is exploited and its people gone, they are gone for ever. Animals, plants and birds are put on lists as endangered species. How much more endangered is a tribe like the Záparo that has only one old woman left? Or the Wagrani, now reduced to a mere five hundred?

Sam is also concerned about what happens after the oil has been used up and Quito has taken its fill of the Oriente. Will the land then revert to his people? Will they be there to receive it?

As always with Sam, his conversation returns to the missionaries. He is a product of their creation, but when they took him on, they did not know they were taking a jaguar by the tail. He says that they have given his tribe medicine* and that they care for the needs of today with no thought for the morrow. 'They have taken the group and changed its way of life – for what? Who will replace the little they have given when they leave, as they say they must, soon? All that will be left will be a copy of the Bible in Wagrani. The people can't live on that. They have given them "Faith". But whose faith? They have moved all the people to one area. Yes, my mother chose it, but she has no authority either. On whose authority have all these people been moved around the jungle?'

Glen Turner, a slight, lean man with a slow, cautious voice, so soft that it is difficult to hear him, was Director of Indian Affairs for the Summer Institute of Linguistics in Ecuador. He has been in the country as long as Rachel Saint, and long ago completed the task set him: the translation of the New Testament into Shuar. He and Don Johnson, Director of SIL, have a difficult job walking the tightrope between the different pressures of their work as they see it, as

---

* The SIL–Voz Andes Hospital at Limoncocha charges for all medicine at full cost. The Capuchin hospitals at Coca and Rocafuerte charge working people: the rest receive free medicine.

the government sees it, as anthropologists and conservationists such as Survival International see it, as left-wing political elements see it, as the World Council of Churches sees it, and as Sam sees it.

The SIL find it difficult to answer their critics. Don Johnson said, 'These people say, "My mind is made up; don't confuse me with facts." They won't listen to any other viewpoint.'

Glen Turner's opinion was that most of the critics of SIL were left-wing revolutionaries, who see revolution as their only answer and the work of the SIL as being right-wing, and standing in their way. They quote the Geneva-based World Council of Churches as an example. The World Council of Churches does not support any Wycliffe or SIL activity although, according to both Donald Johnson and Glen Turner, the WCC supports and finances guerrilla activities in Africa, and has, in fact, recently given a grant of £45,000 to the Rhodesian guerrillas who massacred the families of British missionaries in 1978.

The World Council of Churches also supported the conclusion of the Barbados Conference of 1971 which concludes that: 'As a result of this analysis we conclude that the suspension of all missionary activity is the most appropriate policy for the good of Indian society and for the moral integrity of the churches involved. Until this objective can be realized the missions must support and contribute to Indian liberation.'

Donald Johnson said he would have sympathy with all the points raised in the Barbados Declaration if they were at all applicable to the way in which the SIL conducted themselves.

'We have a consideration of the realities,' he said. 'There are pressures on the indigenous cultures which have nothing to do with evangelical organizations. They were there before we ever came. When large numbers of people of dominant cultures move in, the Indians suffer. Laws are set up under which they have no rights. The whites have all the rights. Laws passed in the capitals have no application to the realities of the Indian groups, and where they clash, the whites get all the benefits.'

He explained that the SIL came to Ecuador to do a job; to record and analyse the unknown tongues of the Oriente, of which Auca was just one. When that work was done they would leave. Their estimate had been fifteen more years, but they hoped to cut that down to half. People were under the impression that the SIL stayed permanently with a primitive tribe, but that was not so. They attempted to train the indigenous populations themselves to continue God's work.

'We haven't made much difference to the exploitation of the Oriente,'

Glen Turner said. 'The substructure of expansion and exploitation was there long before we came and will continue long after we have left. People say that the Indians have got along all right with their fears, with all their warfare, but we know that in time this would have come pretty close to decimating the population. We aim to prevent that. People have also said that we have taken germs in from the outside. We can't deny that, but the whole business of isolation today is realistic only in certain areas and in certain times and in the present time (as of 1978) the areas in which this can be maintained are almost nil, even in the vast expanses of Brazil, and it's these demographic pressures that require consideration of the Indian problem by the lawmakers.'

The SIL define the Indian problem as being the problem that comes in any culture contact. It is a problem of pressure to change particular people in certain ways, and especially where there is a highly dominant culture which has the power to put rather extreme pressures on the less dominant – the Indian – 'It's a very real problem.'

They feel that the ideal solution, if there is such a thing, can only come where there are ideal men, women and children on both sides. Since there is no such thing, the ideal solution cannot be achieved. What the SIL seek to do is to get the kind of solution which produces the best end results for all concerned. A beneficial compromise, in effect.

The SIL see the future for the Indians of the Oriente as one where the Indians are able educationally to decide for themselves what their way of life is going to be. They say that certain groups will adapt to the dominant culture and other groups will fiercely maintain their own ways.

'This is our position for the Aucas,' said Don Johnson. 'This is where we disagree with Sam at this point. Now I don't know what he says philosophically, or what he sees for the people, or what he's doing out there. Developing tourism and making museum pieces of the Aucas from all accounts.'

Glen Turner said that in his opinion Sam was making museum pieces of a tribe who are some of the world's most accomplished beggars, ready to kill if they don't have their particular needs and wants satisfied.

Don Johnson said the whole organization regretted that Sam had turned his back on Rachel and on the job they were certain he was intended for; to be a missionary and teacher to his people.

'I know that Sam wants us to leave the Aucas. Well, we'll be ready to leave when God tells us to go.'

Sam strode along the streets of Quito through the rain holding hot packages close under his traditional wool jacket. Huge holes gaped from unfinished road-works, pavements were at awkward angles uptilted by the roots of trees.

'It's a more dangerous situation here than in the jungle,' Sam said. 'Every street has a man-trap. In the jungle, things are simple, just anacondas, maybe a jaguar or two. Here in the city you really have to watch out.'

He walked past flowering trees and gross-trunked palms. Lights cloud-muted on the soaring mountains enfolded the high city. Sam in blue jeans, feet pointed out; his movements economical, smooth. He is not tall. Slim, shoulders wide, strong, arched neck. White teeth, lips wide-curved, warm, expressive. His eyes hood secretly, then crinkle in humour. A deep furrow ridges vertically between his brows above the bridge of his nose. Early paintings of North American Indian braves show a similar furrow. He has a quick lizard's blink, a long sliding sideways glance that without words conveys a depth of meaning.

Sam and Christina held open house in Quito. At times they refused to answer the bell. When they did there was a constant stream of visitors who sat on cushions on the polished wood floor. Long couches accommodated overnight guests. Spears, blowpipes, basketwork, feather head-dresses of his people decorated the white walls. A circular black and white print over the gothic grey stone fireplace became white angels or black devils, bats, penises, or vaginas with every flicker of the flames. Wool blankets, hand-woven fabrics, fans of rare black coral from the Galapagos Islands, single flowers in little glass vases, books in various languages, records and tapes, were scattered on every surface.

Christina made tea and set out the tea things with precise care on the straw mat before the fire. Wooden platters were used for the still-hot meats brought in by Sam. Her hair was damp from the rain and sparkled red in the flames. She unzipped long, brown leather boots, peeled off baby-blue bed socks and sat, lotus position, on a cushion before the fire.

Friends drifted in. A tall blond young American pilot whose name is John. 'The only good conscription and Vietnam did me was to teach me to fly.' He worked in the oil fields of the Napo and his job paid for his boat moored at Panama. He and Sam talked of sailing it down to Ecuador and taking a trip to the Galapagos.

Two French-Canadians, travellers. The girl was gentle with loose light-brown hair. She wore a long patchwork skirt and thong sandals. The boy was bearded and quiet. They sat on the floor and murmured in French. 'Quebec is French. We are French. But it is not good that we don't speak English. Without languages you are isolated.'

Joey, with shining, short, dark, bobbed hair, huge brilliant black eyes and long sweeping lashes. Impossible eyes, they light up her face. She makes clothes from local fabrics and has a small clientele. Her American parents came to Ecuador in the first rush of the oil boom.

'I don't understand why the people of the Oriente can't make a good living,' she said. 'There is so much there. All that fruit and fish and game. It's teeming with life. It must be the richest land in the world.'

'No, it's not like that,' said Sam. 'The soil is poor. Really poor. It's hard work living in the jungle, I'm telling you. A lot of nonsense is talked about Paradise, but Paradise was hard too. Even there, food had to be found and shelters built.'

Joey described the art of cock-fighting. Her brother-in-law kept fighting birds, so she understood its finer points. Cock-fighting by its very nature illustrates all the Latin male characteristics.

Macho is the absolute in Latin masculinity. A man can be really poor but will never clean his own shoes. He'll always find three *sucres* and sit in the street like a king on his throne and have a child grovel at his feet. Even the fact that the polish is applied with bare hands is in itself a required act of submission.

Sam told a story about the sense of smell he developed in the jungle. 'You can smell a man some distance away,' he said. 'I can even smell hearts.' He laughed with his eyes and produced a pack of cards and showed them a whole range of card tricks, which he learned in college. He is good.

John the pilot asked Sam about his people.

Sam said, 'Folks say that going on a journey to my people must be like going to the end of the world. But it's like going on a journey to the beginning of the world. It's how it was, right at the start when the world was young and man uncomplicated. It's basic living there with no trimmings.'

17

A Recent Journey to Sam's Rio Cononaco Wagrani Group

ON A HIGH HILL within the sprawling city and overlooking the new part of Quito is an oval-fronted pale yellow building. The road is steep, guarded by soldiers. Large letters stretch along the curved front at roof level proclaiming 'Instituto Geografico Militar'.

The view from the roof is breathtaking, showing the close mountain ranges that surround the city which seems suspended in the sky. Strangers find the thin pure air difficult at first, and altitude sickness is common. Quito is over nine thousand feet above sea level, but the snow-capped peaks ries even higher into the vivid blue sky.

Pichincha, Antisana, Cotopaxi. There is a flavour of magic about their legendary names. To the east, beyond the volcanoes of Cotopaxi and Antisana, lies the Amazon rain forest. In those mountains rise the tributaries of the Amazon, falling in swift clear cataracts to become looping yellow ochre rivers, forming a pattern of fat anacondas lying sluggish in the green bed of the jungle.

The new city and newer airport lie to the north. It is a long, narrow conglomeration, forced to follow the confines of the long, narrow Central Valley. Tall office blocks, marble hotels, wide streets, imaginative statues and hopeless plumbing. It has all mushroomed up within the last ten years from what were fertile farms on the volcano-rich soil. Concrete companies and sanitation engineers are making fortunes but are unable to cope with the boom. Telephone, lighting and sewerage companies have very nearly given up the unequal struggle. There is no postal delivery, and taxi drivers are constantly bemused by streets that simply were not there yesterday.

To the south is the old city, pink and blue and white houses running up and down low hills, looking delightful and smelling dreadful. A massive and vulgar silver angel with a hint of the Virgin Mary and a halo of unholy stars dominates one hill, the old city, the pestilential bus station, and the overflowing sewage works.

The bus station lies on the outskirts and is permanently covered with a haze of dust, churned up in the layer of yellow clay which covers the rocks close to the surface. The ground has never been levelled, except by the wheels of the country buses which are painted in brilliant colours, loaded as much on the outside as inside and decorated with paper flowers and plastic Virgins.

An old woman from Otavalo sat in the dust, her white enamel buckets crawling with flies and filled with salted maize and papaya juice. She wore a cerise wool shawl and orange jumper over a dark-red felt skirt. A bib of red beads covered the front of her jumper. Her felt hat was brown, and a long pig-tail hung down her back. She sucked one half of an orange dry, then squeezed the juice from the other half into the bowl of the sucked half. A small child crawled in the dust playing with a white three-legged puppy. The woman finished her orange and removed the dirty pants from the child whose behind was raw and peeling. She cleaned the child with the pants, then wiped her nose with a corner of the grey garment.

The cobbles were full of fish-heads and silver beer-bottle tops. Rows of petrol drums, sliced in half vertically and filled with beds of coals, offered portions of sucking-pig, chicken, roast potatoes and pimento. A lorry passed, spraying the vendors and their food with thick black fumes.

The bus to the cloud forest town of Puyo, a hundred miles away, was ready to leave and moved off, past the open sewage works and rubbish dump, scoured over by bands of small children and dogs, to the hill that winds up to the head of the valley and the mountain road to Cotopaxi.

Small houses and wooden shacks lined the road once the outskirts of the town were passed. Patchwork quilts and knitted blankets aired on wicker fences and rows of washing hung between the houses. The front doors of the colour-washed cottages stood open, exposing baked earth floors on which children and animals played.

A storm was brewing and the high mountains changed colour as rapidly and dramatically as the sky. As the road climbed higher, the long, forward-running ridges were profiled against the navy-blue wooded mountain ridges and black, jagged peaks. White haciendas in the far distance seemed lost in a sea of waving grass and clear light.

Chimiborazo was passed. The brilliant white snow-peak stood stark and ravishing against the sky. Thick grey snowclouds filled the valley below. The mountain's yellow-grey lower slopes were blue with new plantations of eucalyptus.

Now the bus travelled through the high horse country where ranches stretched as far as the eye could see, the long grass rippling and hazy, the trees merging and floating as if the whole range were a sea.

The cows in the Spanish haciendas grazed well on sweet mountain grass; those of the Indians were tethered by short leads to odd pockets of grass along the roadside and in the ditches.

The Indians seemed careless of their safety as they walked along the grass banks, and frequent small white crosses at the roadside pointed in mute evidence to this. At the site of each one there had occurred a fatal accident. The name and date was painted in black.

The bus slowed, then stopped to avoid a small cluster of people. On the road was a long red-black salami, wrapped in a coarse brown cloth; only it wasn't a salami. There were toes on one end. With a shock of horror, a body was seen, several yards away, the blood still pooling out from the severed stump. Another white cross.

It could have been Wales, or Yorkshire or Switzerland, but for the volcanoes and the Indian women in their vivid clothes and jewellery, and the men in ponchos and white cotton trousers. Both men and women wore felt trilbies in a whole range of colours. There were new pine plantations covering the moors, and in the distance the new NASA* station. People lived here in triangular ridge tents made of brown canvas stretched over pine poles through which the wind blew freely. Little piles of grass also turned out to be homes for the Indians.

As the bus now hurtled round the giddy bends into the valley beyond Cotopaxi, a desert landscape developed. The fields were divided by cacti and prickly-pear and the tall flowering yucca. The houses looked like haystacks, and the haystacks were thatched with red tiles. The police post in the middle of nowhere to check the identity of travellers was surrounded by a garden of pansies. Buffeted by high winds, the bus tore frantically round the bends, heading for every precipice. An Australian landscape unfolded: deep orange gorges, cacti, eucalyptus trees and sheep. The earth was now bare but for clumps of flowers and pampas grass. Distant snows sparkled against the vivid sky.

As the sun fell, the clouds around the volcano Tungurahua turned orange and then it was dark in Baños, where the mountains rose in a sheer wall all

* North American Space Agency.

around. Here were mineral springs and sugar cane and great vats of bubbling syrup. Spun-sugar confections were on sale. The women stir the copper bowls of syrup with poles, and chat and dip twigs in to pull the candy out.

The road from Baños through the cloud forest to Shell Mera follows the headwaters of the Pastaza River along the walls of a precipice past the thundering Agoyan falls. Insects and huge night-flying moths flew into the bus as it bumped and swayed inches from the edge of the cliff that fell away hundreds of feet to the moonlit valley below.

At Shell Mera, Captain William Flores was waiting to fly out to the far reaches of the Oriente where Sam had returned to stay with an isolated group of his people.

Captain Flores was one of the first members of the Ecuadorian Air Force and he pioneered civil aviation over the jungle. He lives at Macas, a jungle town fifteen minutes away by air but two days' journey by road. There is no direct road. Travellers have to go from Shell Mera to the coast, and back towards the Andes from the Peruvian border. Macas was built by the Spanish four hundred and fifty years ago as an outpost in Jivaro territory. The Jivaros are head-hunters, the people of the sacred waterfalls. The land around Shell Mera is rich in legend, and most archaeological sites have not yet been examined. An extensive tea plantation, for example, grows over thirty-three distinctive mounds of an ancient settlement or burial ground.

Captain Flores's wife was with him. She had been shopping in Quito. Her nickname is Negra – 'Blackie'. Her servant, a Shuar Indian, told her the story of a strange bird with a hard shell back that guards the Lake of the Sacred Waterfall. It flies at all trespassers and sucks the blood from their chest. This serving-maid described how she was hypnotically lured to a lagoon deep in the forest where she saw a many-headed anaconda which rose from the water and waved its body as she walked closer and closer. She screamed and some Indians ran to her aid. The snake dived, the ground shook, and the water turned black. Negra Flores questioned them all, and they all confirmed that this was so.

Another of her servants declared that a snake was drinking milk from her breast at night, and putting its tail into the baby's mouth to pacify it. When the woman woke and saw the snake, the household was roused. The snake let go of her breast and escaped. It was hunted for two days, and was finally killed when it returned for more milk.

Dr Norman Whitten, ethnologist at the University of Illinois who was staying at the Hostel Turingio at Puyo while doing field-work in Shuar territory, said such legends were common among Christianized natives.

Like Alice in the Australian outback, Shell Mera (Pastaza as it is called locally) is 'a cow of a place', and in fact cows' hoof soup is a favourite dish. On one side is the airfield and the soldiers guarding against Peruvian invaders, and on the other a long single row of ugly houses, with a raised sidewalk. The road is unpaved and as heavy lorries thunder by the earth vibrates as if it is hollow and the houses frequently collapse.

Puyo is at the end of the road a few kilometres away. The jungle encroaches from all sides, Puyo's sounds and smells are of the jungle, and it appears to be waiting either for civilization to catch up with it, or for the jungle to reclaim it. It is shabby or romantic, depending on the eye of the beholder.

The onward journey by air was impossible for three days. The land is not called the cloud forest for nothing, and travellers sometimes have to wait anything up to a week for the cloud cover to lift. They pass the time by walking up and down the main street at Shell Mera, drinking cold beer and consuming hoof soup and mountains of rice, aji sauce and boiled potatoes. The diet is heavily biased in favour of carbohydrates.

The house where Nate and Marj Saint used to live is on the outskirts of the town, a house built with their own hands; originally a wood and corrugated-iron shack, but at the time Nate Saint died it had been expanded into a ten-bedroomed colonial-type bungalow, and today is the finest house in the whole area, with well-kept lawns and bushes crowned with feathery pink flowers like the crest on a crowned crane. Rachel Saint took cuttings to Tiwaeno.

Next door are six red and white MAF (Missionary Aviation Fellowship) planes – in Nate Saint's day they were yellow – and near by the spacious HJCB* hospital staffed by attractive Americans, many of whom donate their time. HJCB is the missionary broadcasting station in Quito. Its director became Marj Saint's second husband. HJCB is undoubtedly the most powerful radio station in the world and claims it can transmit to 'the uttermost parts of the earth'. Its very size has led to the charge that it is a cover for the CIA as no missionary radio station needs to be so powerful. What people do not realize is the obsessive desire of the missionary associates to reach out to everyone with the word of God.

---

* Called Voz Andes in Ecuador ('Voice of the Andes').

18

Experiences on the Cononaco with Sam

SAM HAS BEEN CRITICIZED FOR giving the Wagrani something that helps rot their teeth, but in November 1977, six oil company workers were speared to death in the Ridge area by recalcitrant Wagrani from the Ridge group, who then turned on members of their own tribe and caused old fears to mount.

Sam was called in by Texaco-CEPE to go and talk to them, to try to dissuade them from creating further havoc.

The killers were no longer there, but the remaining members of the tribe were nervous about the future. Sam told them of a place he knew in the south, far away from the Ridge, on the Cononaco River. He had first been there as a guide for the oil companies. An airstrip was built but no oil was found and the site was abandoned. Sam described its advantages, the wide river, the untouched game, and the distance it would put between them and the killers. So they put their worldly goods into their *chigras* and like the children of Israel, wandered off to a new home.

No Wagrani had ever lived there and there were no crops, so Sam flew in ahead with supplies of rice, beans and sugar. He took the sugar, he said, 'because I reckoned they would need the extra energy. It would take them time to locate wild banana.'

Half the group went on ahead to see what the place was like while the others, more cautious, remained at the Ridge, but the authorities were not happy at still having a group of killer Indians on their doorstep. With the co-operation of the military and SIL, ninety Wagrani were whisked away from the Ridge to the Protectorate zone, leaving their Cononaco relatives wondering where they had gone. Sam, waiting on the Cononaco River for them, was unaware that they had been diverted to the Protectorate zone, and thought they might have lost themselves. He hired an aeroplane and searched the vast expanse of jungle looking for them. 'If I had known they were all sitting in Tiwaeno, I would have saved my money,' he said.

He wrote to the SIL asking them to return the people whence they had come. There was no reply.

In Quito, Don Johnson and Glen Turner's explanation was that the Ridge people had asked to be taken to Tiwaeno where many of their relatives lived. 'Families were divided, we united them,' Don Johnson said.

Sam goes frequently to the Cononaco, and the people built him a house as a surprise. 'I don't know why I don't live here,' he said. 'This place refreshes me. I get jaded in Quito. Spend too much money. Life is complicated. I feel at peace here with these folk.'

The Wagrani on the banks of the Cononaco wear no clothes, only their kumi belts. Their bodies are compact and firmly muscled, and the younger ones have unconscious grace in every movement. Some of them are affected by an intestinal worm, and have huge stomachs. It is difficult to tell which of the women are pregnant and which are not.

They have a warm, candid gaze, and crowd around, laughing uproariously, and touching, patting, entwining fingers. Every inch of a stranger is explored and exclaimed upon. They have a particular interest in ears, breasts, genitals, nails. Red polish on toe-nails confused them, and they examined the foot to see where the wound was. A blister on the heel was also looked at with interest and their own heels looked at in comparison.

There was a rainbow in the sky, but the Wagrani did not point to it. They believe that to do so brings a pain in the elbow. They say that at the end of the rainbow is found the best clay from which they make their cooking pots – an interesting variation on the crock of gold theme.

Their pots are a unique shape, being far narrower at the bottom than at the top. Aluminium pots are used, especially for carrying water, but the clay pot is always used for cooking monkey meat. They are made by building them up from long rolls of clay. They are smoothed down, first by hand, and then with a curved piece of gourd or shell, and left close to a fire or in the sun until they dry out. Next they are placed in the centre of a smoking pyre of green wood for several hours. No glaze or decoration is applied, but the minerals in the clay produce a delicately glazed effect. The pots are very fragile and do not last long.

From Sam's house on a low bluff above the river, the trail to the two main

houses where thirty Wagrani live crosses a narrow stream and proceeds up a
steep path in which footholds have been shaped by the repetitive placing of
many feet. The clearing at the top was reached, and there in all his fierce
splendour was the harpy eagle, sacred guardian of the people. Although held
captive on his high perch, with his fine crest and curved beak he looked wild
and free outlined against the blue and white sky.

Men returned from their hunt carrying many spider-monkeys killed by
curare darts shot from blowguns. The curare affects the nerves controlling the
muscles. If a live animal is wanted, the amount of curare used is limited. Small
doses of the poison do not affect humans, but in any case, its potency is rendered
harmless by cooking.

The monkeys were singed over fires to remove their thick fur, and jointed
quickly and efficiently with a heavy-bladed knife. The raw meat was dark red,
almost purple, and it was shared out, the best parts going to the family of the
hunter, the tail, belly flaps and entrails to the families of two sick men unable
to hunt. A hind-quarter, one of the best parts, was given to the eagle. The meat
portions were closely packed in water in the large clay 'monkey pots', and banana
leaves tied down over the top of them with vine. After about an hour over the
fire it was cooked. It tasted delicious, somewhat like the drumstick of a turkey
and a haunch of venison.

It was the fat monkey season, and great numbers of them were killed every
day. The monkeys fatten up when their favourite foods are in season and they
gorge themselves. Then comes the chonta palm season when the ripe orange
fruit gives them diarrhoea and the fat runs from their bodies, making them lean
and tough.

Everyone went swimming for an hour as the sun set. The way down to the
river was steep, a wall of clay. The children showed great consideration, taking
the white visitors' hands and carrying their soap and clean clothes. The Wagrani
at Cononaco spend nearly all day in the water, playing, fishing, swimming.
The current was strong and in order to cross the wide river they walked upstream and dived in, letting the current carry them across. Their bobbing dark
heads and luminous eyes gave them the appearance of seals.

On a green moss-covered bank, a small trickle of water fell down to the
river. The entire wall and ledge beneath it were thickly covered in butterflies
absorbing both moisture and the last rays of the sun.

There were over a dozen different large varieties, their many-coloured wings
overlapping and fanning each other. The hot jungle night fell. There would
be a storm later, and there were no stars, no moon.

It rained in the night. A great storm. The chambira palm hammocks were comfortable, but it became very cold in the early hours of the morning. Sam used a blanket but the Wagrani slept naked, curled up together around their low fires. The mist was still heavy in the morning when the first silent Wagrani crept into Sam's house like the river mist and stood impassively for over an hour, quietly waiting. When Sam indicated that he was awake, they broke into animated conversation as they touched and patted his white friends.

'They are asking if you had a good night; if you slept well,' Sam explained.

The girls ran down to the river for fresh water and the men, who had seen that the palm-thatch had leaked in the night, swam across the river to get fresh leaves. The leaves, which were dark green and forked, were woven into the roof and the fork was bent over the rafters to keep them in place.

Everyone helped, swarming up the main posts. The women picked up the leaves with their dexterous big toe and handed them up to the men who also caught them with their toes - a facility which will be lost as the Wagrani become civilized and wear shoes, like those at Tiwaeno.

In everything they did, in their looks, touches, smiles and helpfulness, the people were warm and friendly, and it was difficult to relate this tactile awareness and consideration with their long tradition of spearing and abandoning their babies. It was difficult to feel fear in their presence, yet everyone had said how dangerous it was, out there on the Cononaco.

'They still abandon kids if they have too many,' Sam said. 'That man there,' and he nodded to one of the men busy repairing the roof, 'got rid of a kid last month. He had three girls; she was a fourth. He says he is waiting for a son next time. Someone to help in hunting.'

When Sam was asked about spearing, he said that many of the older men in the group had killed enemies in the past - the quite recent past - but their attitude now was that it was better to live without killing. He was asked if that was because they had listened to Rachel Saint.

'None of them have met Rachel Saint,' Sam said. 'They came from the Ridge and have never been to Tiwaeno.' He paused. 'They say that they only killed each other for revenge. It was something which had to be done. Now that there hasn't been a killing for some time - at least, not in the tribe - there are no more revenges left. They will kill outsiders, they say, if the outsiders take anything from them, or threaten their freedom.' Sam shrugged. 'Maybe they will, maybe they won't. These guys haven't killed for a long time and don't seem too keen on starting again.'

That explanation of why people who had killed traditionally for centuries should suddenly cease did not seem to fit the facts. If these people had never been in contact with Rachel Saint, who had seemed able to change many things,

A Wagrani - here with spear, blowgun and new darts - hunts to survive. His protein rich diet builds solid muscles and keeps him healthy. Game is plentiful outside the overhunted Protectorate, but in critical supply within it

The nerve-stunning poison, curare, is made from the bark of a vine, scraped with flint or sharp shell onto a palm leaf, which is then bound into a funnel. Water is spat from the mouth, and drips for several hours into a ritual gourd. The dark-brown liquid is heated slowly over a fire – traditionally in a clay pot, but here in an aluminium gift kettle – until a viscous scum forms, which is scraped up with a dart and mixed on a flat stone. Darts are dipped in the poison, then smoked in a fan pattern until they are hard

RIGHT: Blow guns are very heavy, made of iron-wood, the two hollowed halves stuck together with beeswax, then bound with vines. Note the poison gourd container and dart case hanging in front.

OVERLEAF: Decorating spears with macaw feathers on the Cononaco – used to kill each other as well as game

LEFT: Home from the hunt with spider monkeys – recognizable by their long arms. They are meaty and taste like venison – every part is eaten.

RIGHT: The whole animal is charred over a fire until they look like sooty babies and jointed (bottom left) then boiled in plain water in the special 'monkey pot' over which banana leaves are placed.
FAR RIGHT: the head is a great treat, and is chewed and sucked for hours

many of the old ways, then what was it that had caused such a dramatic and basic moral improvement?

Sam seemed reluctant to define it. Possibly he had not thought about it in wider terms and Sam will never form an opinion unless he has facts; but there had to be an answer to explain why we were there, in peace and confidence, in a group of so-called savage killers.

During the nights of story-telling, during the moments when newcomers arrived and others packed their *chigras* and took their pets to vanish without a word into the jungle, the answer came: Toña.

Toña was dead and his body long decayed and picked over by the vultures, not even given the benefit of a Wagrani burial – but in the months he had spent on the Ridge, this quiet and intelligent man had brought home, in his simple way, the message taught him by Rachel Saint.

Wagrani know nothing of the Western message and history of the Bible. The circumstances of Christ's birth and death have no meaning to them. Descriptions of miracles, seas, angels, asses, temples, are more remote to their understanding than the aeroplanes that pass overhead. But they do have a God, a heaven and a hell. If 'God' is explained to them, in their own terms, they can understand.

The Bible stories, in their own terms, can be appreciated. Rachel Saint noticed, as she grew more fluent in Wag, that when Dayuma told the people the stories that she herself had been taught, she always converted them to suit the audience. At times this bothered Rachel and those to whom she was answerable, believing as they did that the dogma in the Bible is absolute, but she had to become philosophical about it, assuring herself that later, with education, the Wagrani would learn the actual facts and the true version of the New Testament stories.

Toña had been taught by Rachel, but like Dayuma, he translated her lessons into easily digestible morsels and related everything in jungle terms. The Wagrani love stories. They tell them at every opportunity and it is in this way that their legends and news is passed on where there is no other method of recording things. It does not take long for a new story to be absorbed into the culture and to become part of the repertoire of the story-tellers. Toña had authority and he was sincere. His stories carried weight, and although he himself was killed in a gesture of rebellion by Wepe's supporters, his stories lived on.

Rachel Saint herself was, and still is, unaware of the full extent of this transformation amongst people she has never met, but there can be no other reasonable explanation for this transformation, for this affection for total strangers and

TOP: A small lake contains countless piranha – fishermen keep their distance from a fish that in schools will attack any mammal, including man. BOTTOM RIGHT: the delicious piranha weigh up to 2 lbs – hooks are curved bits of shell, line is made from vine string. BOTTOM LEFT: Standing on a submerged log in the river, where fishing is done with nets

for the consideration shown them at all times.

The combination of primitive simplicity and naturalness with this candid love is an astonishing and moving thing. One feels that the more sophisticated people in the world, not of the jungle, with their greed, politics, religious wars, socialist envy and capitalist ruthlessness should take a look at what civilization has done. These are emotional thoughts and very little will change the world, and there are always people who cry in the wilderness; but nevertheless, in the middle of the Amazon jungle, in the midst of a stone-age people, one can, for a moment, forget the world, and for a moment, wish that life could stand still.

People say that going into the jungle is a cultural shock; one is warned about it. Coming back into so-called civilization is an even greater one. The Aucas who were jetted around the world must have gone into a state approaching shell-shock that no Westerner could have really appreciated. No wonder Rachel Saint fought against taking them away from the jungle on tours, even for a brief period. Had her organization the right to demand it?

Rachel Saint's words are recalled: 'Life outside seems to be so complicated, so full of unnecessary pressures. I like nothing about it.'

Still, the jungle is not all the stuff that Eden was made of. The Wagrani do still kill – outsiders, if not themselves or each other. Sam was asked about the deaths of the six oil company workers the previous November.

'They say that the oil men were warned for seven days. They put spears across the trail each morning, but the warning was ignored. They didn't want a road right into their territory like that. It threatened them. These guys weren't the ringleaders and knew nothing about it until later. They say the killers enjoy killing now and won't stop.'

It was from these killers that the group on the Cononaco made their escape to the very limits of their territory. It was from these same killers that the SIL airlifted other members to Tiwaeno, causing a certain amount of resentment in Sam and family members on the Cononaco.

During the evenings there was frequent discussion. Where was this person, or that person? Were they dead? Where had they gone? Why had they not come as they said they would?

The questions circled back and forth, and Sam was unable to answer; he had not, at that point, been to Tiwaeno to see for himself.

There are people who believe that the Wagrani have a right to kill outsiders in order to protect their territory. It is, after all, no more than is expected of the major powers when their territory is threatened and invaded. Have these people less right to their land than America to hers, or Russia to hers?

One anthropologist from Princeton is still talked of with some amusement and a certain degree of respect in Quito. He came to study the Aucas, saw what was happening, and lumping missionaries, oil men and settlers into one aggressive force, decided to redress the balance. He hired a helicopter, loaded up with mysterious packages, and flew over some Auca houses, dropping his packages. They happened to contain rifles and ammunition, which afforded him enormous satisfaction. He left the country on the first plane, while the row raged in his wake. The missionaries still refuse to talk about it.

19

Rachel Saint in Quito Today

FOR TWENTY YEARS RACHEL SAINT had lived in Tiwaeno amongst the Wagrani as friend, teacher and nurse.

She rarely left the jungle. The work always seemed to need her constant attention and she felt that the people had learned to trust her and this growing relationship was a very fragile flower in the early days, only too easily broken. The jungle weaves a spell on those who live there. Distances recede and time expands. What importance can there possibly be in the election of a new president, or a mugging in Buffalo, when one is so close to the mysteries of nature?

Rachel described what it meant to her.

'It is the only place on earth where I'm never lonely. It is my home and those people are my family in a very real sense. I have been there so long that I don't really understand the outside world any more.'

Rachel Saint's base for her work in Tiwaeno has been Limoncocha, a large settlement on the banks of the Napo River. Limoncocha (Lime Lagoon) is also the base for all Summer Institute of Linguistics operations in the northern jungle, and is a most unexpected sight. It is like an American park, with mown lawns, flowering shrubs and trees, neat gardens and trim houses that look as if they have been lifted straight from a Hollywood set; they are spacious, cool and airy, wood-walled and crisply thatched. There is electricity, piped water, air conditioning and enormous refrigerators. Furniture is light, simple and comfortable, made at the base carpenters' shop where local Indians are taught how to use the wood all about them, and so earn a living.

Here American agriculturalists experiment with crops and livestock that will survive in the jungle while visiting scientists study, in comfort, jungle life as it sweeps in to the very edges of the base. Linguists can see for themselves the people whose language they are studying, Bible students can see missionary work in action; there are doctors, nurses, dentists, teachers and a modern clinic.

The establishment is so big that the linguists ride around on beach buggies. A DC 3 arrives from Quito twice a week with fresh supplies and visitors. The river people, whoever they are from Catholic missionaries to traders, drop in to hitch a lift to Quito. The drone of the heavy-duty generators merely serves to pace the constant activity.

Although Rachel had a small thatched house of her own at Limoncocha, she used it as little as possible. One has the distinct impression that she considers the work done at Limoncocha 'soft' in comparison with the real spear-heading work done in the depths of the jungle. Life in Tiwaeno has always been very hard – she has always felt as if she were walking on a razor's edge.

'Although it is now a Christian settlement many of the surrounding Auca tribes are still very hostile. Even at Tiwaeno I am with people for whom killing has long been a way of life. They are Stone Age Indians. You can't expect them to change their instincts overnight.'

When asked how she felt about being in daily contact with the men who killed her brother, the question seemed to surprise her.

'I believe it was God's will that Nate should die. He made my work here possible. Without his sacrifice they would never have seen the light. And how can you possibly feel bitterness towards men who have the minds of children? I don't hate Kimo and his fellow spear-throwers of Palm Beach. I love them. They are, in a very real sense, part of my family.'

To spend twenty years in such an environment is a remarkable sacrifice, but Rachel certainly doesn't look on it like that. She says that she was able to live in Tiwaeno for so long through God's grace. 'I myself am nothing. My authority comes from God and I am a very humble servant of his and of these people who are my friends. I am here with God's grace and their permission and invitation. Before I could come in Dayuma asked them, then came out to fetch me back with her. She guided me in, and I am here with her protection and friendship. And I know that it is all the will of God; it has nothing to do with my courage or my recklessness or with anything else that makes me look brave or important.

'I get frightened like anyone else. I know, better than most, what a terrible weapon a barbed spear can be. It can be a slow and agonizing way to die. Sometimes I dream about such a death, and wake shaking in the night. I am realistic enough to know that I have been very fortunate to have survived out here so long. And I suppose the chances are that one day I will be speared to death. It could happen so very easily. But, you see, although I am afraid of dying, I don't fear death itself, and this is my great comfort.'

Today Rachel Saint lives in Quito in a small room of the modern buildings of the Summer Institute of Linguistics.

From the balcony she can see the great mountains that divide the Sierra, the long central valley of the high Andes, from the jungle. All around the new buildings of the expanding town crowd in; one can literally see them grow. Workers are perched on the typical wooden scaffolding that not only looks dangerous, but is. Directly in front of Rachel's front door, just across the lawns, a building collapsed, killing all the workmen. It is still a pile of rubble.

When she first came to Quito with the nucleus of the SIL, their land was set in acres of meadows filled with wild flowers. The near-by airport, now a busy international centre, was a field with a converted cowshed at one end.

Rachel Saint stood on her balcony and waved her arm at the expanding city.

'All this has happened in less than twenty years. I find it hard to believe.'

She also finds it hard to believe that she is living in Quito when she wants to be back in the jungle. She has been told that she must stay in Quito in order to complete the Bible translation that took her to Tiwaeno originally; that her prime job is that of linguist, not of nurse or social worker.

The SIL say that the people of Tiwaeno must learn to get along without missionaries and outside help once the New Testament has been translated into their tongue. They must learn, once again, to look after themselves and to expect nothing from the outside world, not to be dependent on the Americans who have introduced cattle, new crops, fowl, clothes and medicine, and who made them dependent on those things in the first place.

The linguists are anxious that a line be drawn between helping these people in a positive way and not, at the same time, setting them up as zoo specimens, chiefly for the benefit, they say, of anthropologists, who would like to see nothing changed.

'They would even like to see the old ways of killings continue,' say the linguists. 'Anthropologists are interested only in their studies, not in the very lives and feelings of the people they are studying.'

The anthropologists, of course, don't deny that they would like to see nothing changed, but they say it is because that is the natural way of life of primitive people and that they are substantially happier in the old ways. They also deny the right of anyone to come, uninvited, and teach an alien religion and way of life.

It is an argument and a dilemma so fundamental that agreement will never be reached.

It is also an argument that leaves Rachel Saint a little bored. 'Let them live in the jungle for twenty years, as I have. Let them see the ruthless killings, the misery that it causes, the living without hope, then let them talk of non-interference – if they have the stomach.'

Rachel Saint left the jungle in order to return to the United States for a series of operations on her eyes and for the specialists to assess what damage lead poisoning had done to her body. Neither she nor the doctors have any idea where the lead came from, although it has been suggested that it was the result of living on tinned tuna for twenty years, a non-medical opinion which amuses her.

'Show me anyone who has lived on tinned tuna for twenty years,' she said.

Wherever the lead came from, the prognosis is not good. The doctors have given her three years.

'Three years is not long. I must get my priorities right. I must decide what is important to me, and do it,' she said.

The problem is that Rachel Saint is torn between her duty to her priorities and her personal wishes. She wants to return to Tiwaeno and feels trapped in Quito, but she has tremendous will power and there is little doubt that she will find a good compromise between priorities and desire.

After her operation in America everyone thought that she was to be pensioned off, to complete her translations in retirement. She was told that she would never be going back to South America unless it was as a private citizen, but in fact during her exile in New Jersey, she declared that she would return, even if she had to walk it. A year later, she was back in Quito, looking longingly at the mountains.

'I'm going back to the jungle,' she said. 'That is my home now.'

Talking to Rachel Saint is a fascinating experience. She has a dry, emphatic sense of humour and a sharp, quick tongue. Her vocabulary could be termed salty if it were not so frank and wholesome. Although it is slangy, it is impossible to imagine her using one bawdy or crude word even to describe what she means by 'filth'.

It is her opinion that the world is wallowing in the pit of Sodom and Gomorrah, and that if things do not change fast there is little hope for mankind.

'We're going backwards so fast it makes my head spin,' she said. 'A thing which is pornographic one year is the fashion the next. Women are the worst. They have no dignity left.'

Rachel remembered when Sam was a teenager living in Tiwaeno. She thought it was time he started to read American papers and she spent a long time compiling a list, remembered from her own youth, of what her seven brothers had been allowed to read. Then she sent for the papers, one at a time. As each one arrived it was immediatly crossed off the list.

'It was disgusting, appalling. There was nothing that I could give a growing boy to read. The smut is so invidious that people don't realize they have been contaminated. But when you live out of the world for so long, as I have, then come back into it by means of a newspaper or journal, you see it so clearly like a shock of dirty, cold water.'

Rachel finally decided that the institution of *Time* magazine could not possibly warp Sam's mind. She ordered it.

'I guess I was duped again,' she said. 'It was full of the most blatant pornography. Articles about rape and drug abuse, and even pictures of half-naked women.'

Sam recollected a similar incident when he was asked by Rachel what gift he would like from Quito during one of her trips to work on a book. He selected an album by Tijuana Brass to play on their portable gramophone, but he never got the album, although Rachel did buy it and take it back to Tiwaeno.

The cover showed a South American beauty in a low-cut evening gown and in Rachel Saint's book women did not display themselves in such a way. The record was banned. Sam said that he could not understand her strict rules, but he respects her for them.

'Rachel is no hypocrite. She never deviates one inch, she never compromises,' he said of her.

'The world needs more people to take a stand against low standards,' Rachel said. 'We are human beings, yet we do the most appalling things to our own bodies and souls. I can tell you, this world has gone to pot. Hatred, envy, greed, sexual rottenness. The people who love their neighbour and respect themselves are a tiny percentage. I certainly don't see many of them and I count myself lucky because I spend more time with Christians than do most people. If I have to search for God in this world – what must the standards of most people be like?'

Rachel Saint is neat, brisk, and reminds one of a plump Dutchwoman. She carries herself well and has a straight back, a firm gaze and a remarkably sweet smile. Her eyes from which the sight is fading fast, are a brilliant blue.

Her fair skin has the bloom of perpetual youth, her long grey hair, more blonde than one expects, is coiled on her neck in a plaited bun, and her ankles are as slender as a racehorse's. Her feet are long and slim and her shoes elegant – the type that might be worn by the Queen. On her little finger she wears an antique gold and garnet ring.

People drop in constantly, greeting her with easy friendliness.

She has a gift for Marj Saint, her sister-in-law, now married to the director of Quito's world missionary radio station, HCJB. Maple syrup in a jam-jar, wrapped in a plastic bag. The syrup had leaked, and the whole package sits on a saucer. It turns out that the gift was brought back from America several months before, but Rachel still has not completed her unpacking.

'By the time I finish it, it will be time to return to the jungle,' she says with assurance. She has a great deal more assurance than nearly all the members of SIL, who are convinced that with only one year to go before she is sixty-five and able to retire, she will never return to Tiwaeno.

'I've gained a year I can do without,' Rachel said. 'I thought I was practically sixty-five and I was planning on retiring to Tiwaeno with my pension – if I am lucky enough to get one. But it turns out that I am still only sixty-three, so that scotched those fine ideas. Serves me right. The Lord has his plans for me, and I should listen to them instead of making my own plans.'

Rachel Saint has every confidence in God's provision for her future, however long or short it may be, but at times she quite naturally worries. She has no money of her own and has never been in a position to save. The few legacies she had she spent on the tribe. Her last legacy was $600 from her father, who had been poor all his life and with six living sons and a daughter had little enough to leave anyone. With the money she bought a second-hand radio receiver which Dayuma uses. Her living and travelling expenses over the years have come solely from donations from her church and from offerings.

The SIL have a system of support and income, whereby their parent body, the Wycliffe Bible Translators, have laid down a basic minimum requirement for their members to live on. Those with wives and children get more than do single members, otherwise they all get the same, regardless of their 'hierarchical' position. All of them get a great deal less than they would if they worked outside the mission. There are fully qualified university lecturers, international airline pilots, doctors, dentists, mechanics, nurses. If the donations are more than the basic requirement, the balance is skimmed off the top and used in a central fund. Of the remainder, all of them contribute ten per cent for the upkeep of the mission base itself, which is supported entirely by the people who work there.

Many of the SIL's critics say that the basic pay must be very high, since most

161

of them in Quito live in the best residential area, have one or two cars, and modern equipment.

Rachel Saint apparently has nothing on which to fall back. She has no home of her own except a straw and thatch hut in the jungle. Even her room in the residential block in Quito is on loan. In America she stays with friends, the Adcocks of Huntingdon Valley.

Pensions are not automatic for retired missionaries and one wonders what Rachel Saint will do without savings.

'Pray,' she said, with a slight twinkle. 'I've been taken care of through prayer all my life.'

Rachel Saint's plans for her future are very simple. She intends to complete her New Testament translations, then retire to Tiwaeno for as long as she is not a burden to the tribe.

'Twenty years ago I started out to translate the Bible into Auca. I've been side-tracked by helping the people. It seems I helped them too well, at the sacrifice of my prime work. My translations are way behind. People who started in other languages in other parts of the world years after me have long finished. Now I have to get my priorities right. I have to finish the work I started out to do, the work Nate and the others died for.'

When asked what made her decide to become a missionary there was no hesitation in her reply:

'God has a plan for each and every one of us. If we listen to him, and ask, we will know. I guess I just listened at the right time when he was speaking to me, and I knew. I've been following his way ever since. I believe, too, that my family were specially blest because of my parents.'

One has the feeling that she is very frustrated by her present confinement to the civilized world. There is a glint of steel in her eye when she declares, 'I am going back'.

Donald Johnson, the tall, grey-blond director of the SIL, has a slightly different opinion. He came to Quito when Rachel did and helped set up the jungle base at Limoncocha and knows as much about Indian affairs in Ecuador as anyone.

'Rachel Saint can't stay with these people for ever,' he said. 'They must be self-sufficient. We, as missionaries, are not here to take them over, but to help preserve a written record of their language and customs, and to help them find God through our work. Then we must move on to other fields. We have two thousand tongues to go. In fact, the anthropologists should be grateful for what we are doing. The Amazon jungles are changing now that oil has been discovered. Change is inevitable. There is no doubt at all in my mind that in a few years from now, the Aucas as an isolated people will probably be a thing of the past. We, the linguists, didn't bring the change, although we have been blamed. Oil did. Progress did. What we are doing is seeking to preserve what might soon be a dead language, a dead culture. The anthropologists might one day be thanking us.'

When it is put to Rachel Saint that all her work might be in vain – that her work of the past twenty years will probably end up on the shelf of a museum, she is not concerned by opinion or suggestions that do not come from God. In her own mind she knows she is doing what is expected of her.

'When a people have their own language written down it gives them a sense of identity, of respect,' she said. 'It is important for them to feel that they count.'

When it is suggested that if she had not gone into the jungle others would not have followed, and the people would have been left alone to pursue their own way as they have over the centuries, and so would not have been any the wiser about the written word, Rachel Saint almost snorts.

'Don't you believe it. There is no way that the Auca were going to be left alone. That is a lovely fairy story thought up by preservationists. With oil men and settlers in the jungle, there would have been a blood bath, and I know who would have come off the worst. Within a decade there would have been no Aucas and no language to preserve. These so called do-gooders just don't know what they're talking about. Most of them verbalize at a distance.

'How many of them have been in the jungle for more than a week, if that, and studied the problems? They fly in, do a lightning so-called investigation, then fly out, talking nonsense. You have to live in the jungle and live with the day-to-day problems to know what the problems are. I'm tired of being told their opinions by people who have never been.'

20

Sam Goes to See His Mother

SAM HAD NOT SEEN HIS MOTHER for nearly two years. He asked if a JAARS plane, based at Limoncocha, could fly him to Tiwaeno, but permission was refused. He asked if Dayuma could be flown out to him, and permission was given provided he paid the fare.* At that time, all Sam's money was going on the high cost of flying food to the people on the Cononaco. He suggested that as Dayuma had done a great deal to raise funds for the SIL by her US tour and the missionary books based on her life, they might make a concession in her favour. This was not accepted. What they said was that Dayuma could walk out of the jungle.

Dayuma had, in fact, already done this. She had walked out and taken a bus from Arajuno to Quito. She wanted to talk to Rachel about many things that confused and concerned her. Rachel had left Tiwaeno one morning saying she would be back soon. Dayuma had waited but Rachel had not returned. Then she had a message to say that Rachel was sick. So Dayuma travelled to Quito, a journey she hated, to see her friend.

For some extraordinary reason, Dayuma was not allowed to see Rachel, neither was Rachel informed of her arrival.

Dayuma asked where her son was staying as she wanted a place to stay at. The answer was a shrug.

'He might be abroad; he might be dead. Who knows?'

Sam was in Quito at the time but was out of favour with the SIL because of a newspaper article unflattering to them. When Sam learned that his mother

* About $450.

164

had asked to see him, he enquired why she had not been told of his where-abouts. The reply startled him.

'Because you are living with a woman who is not your wife. Your mother is heartbroken over your behaviour and has turned her back on you.'

Sam pointed out that all his people 'live with women who are not their wives'. Civil wedding ceremonies are not conducted in the jungle.

'I am free to decide if I am a Wagrani who does not marry in church, or a Quitan who does,' said Sam,

The situation was growing more difficult. Dayuma was refused medicine unless she paid for it in advance. When Sam heard of this, he paid her medical bill at Limoncocha, protesting that most of the drugs were supplied free to the mission under donations and aid schemes.

A package was waiting for Dayuma in Quito, sent by a friend she had met in America. This had not been taken to Limoncocha in the weekly JAARS DC3 because she could not pay for its transport. Sam paid this.

'Where is my mother supposed to get all this money?' he asked. 'Does it grow on trees in the jungle? The missionaries are financed in their work. They have fine houses and cars, refrigerators, and kids at boarding school. They have native servants at Limoncocha. My mother helps them in this work. She translates. She and the Wagrani have been on huge fund-raising tours. Her biography has been written and sixty thousand hardback copies sold. Wycliffe own the copyright. Is she not entitled to some consideration and some medicine for her people? What must they do to get it? Beg and be accused of being beggars, or die? Did they need to beg from anyone before the white man went in? All they ever asked was to be left alone. These missionary folks can't have it both ways. They can't be sent money by the good folk of America to help the savages, and then make the savages pay for it. Who does my mother want the medicine for – herself? Is she some kind of drug addict or something? The medicine is there for the Indians. Okay, let the Indians have it.'

The problems seemed to magnify. Sam decided to make the attempt to go and see his mother and find out what was happening.

His arrival at the booming jungle town of Coca, first stage on the difficult journey, coincided with a problem CEPE were having with the Wagrani. He was rather surprised to see the long lobes of Wagrani actually in the dirt streets of Coca. He saw them go into shops with handfuls of money. He saw them drinking beer, a thing they had never done in the past. Alcohol has a potent effect on these men.

It seemed that, so that these men could earn money for items on which they had now become dependent, like clothes and medicine, one particular member of the SIL at Limoncocha, Patricia Kelly, who was 'in charge' of the Aucas in Rachel Saint's absence, had arranged with CEPE to employ Auca workmen in the area of Gabaron on the Ridge, where six oil company men had been killed the previous November. It was thought that if the marauding band of killers saw their own people working on the road, they might be influenced not to make another attack. This, of course, judging from past history, was most unlikely. But the men needed money, so it was agreed. CEPE paid them a wage of $60 a month, which was an average wage in the area for native workers, and provided all their food.

Once some men had been taken from Tiwaeno, others followed, walking out. For the first time in history, a whole group of Aucas roamed through the town. The residents of Coca were astonished once they had got over their initial panic. These Aucas were well-dressed. They looked like humans but for the holes in their lobes. There were no spears in sight.

CEPE wanted Sam to explain to the Aucas that the trail was nearly finished and that soon it would be time for them to go home. In exchange for this service, a helicopter of Equavia Oriente would fly Sam in to the Curaray, where there was no airstrip, to see his mother.

The Aucas in Gabaron were able to communicate with CEPE only through one of their number who had learnt to speak Spanish during his years in an iron lung in Limoncocha after he had contracted polio. He told Sam that it was very difficult explaining many things to the men, and impossible to check that their money was not stolen from them during their shopping trips.

The Oriente is marked off on the oil maps in a series of grids that relate to the flight maps. There are very few landing strips for small aircraft, but heli-copter pads are marked on every square; a helicopter needs about six square feet on which to land, and trees cleared from an area about the size of an average back garden to give it room to manoeuvre. The only drawback of a helicopter is that it has limited range without refuelling, and it was the job of the Wagrani working for CEPE-Texaco to help hack out the landing pads and also the con-necting roads from camp to camp. Exploratory oil rigs need no road, but the minute a strike is made and a well starts producing, the machine age moves in on a wide scale. Roads, camps, pipelines, trucks, storage tanks. Along the new roads, settlers move in and start their stripping and clearing of the trees and rough ploughing of the soil.

As the helicopter flew to where the Wagrani were working, many such settlements were passed and the extent of the jungle clearance could be clearly seen. Then the road ended; at the last camp the helicopter refuelled and the virgin jungle rolled beneath the whirring rotors. The life in the top, canopy layer of the forest was more easily seen, since we were flying far lower than in an aeroplane: the bright patches of bog, plantains and banana, flowering trees, small streams, rounded hills topped with palms, brilliant long-tailed birds. The pilot followed the grid lines on his map and for a moment could not find the newest camp site. It was nearly impossible to see, marked only by a small area of brown, where leaves from felled trees were dying. The trees had not been cleared. They criss-crossed each other in confusion, but there was a six-foot-square slab, made of banana leaves on a branch base. It looked a very unsteady platform on which to land.

Suddenly the clearing was filled with the figures of the Wagrani workers. They wore an odd assortment of ragged clothes and some most inventive hats, from the arm of a tee-shirt, to a paper hat fastened with silver wire. All wore rubber boots. They looked at Sam in frank astonishment. They hadn't seen him for some years and now here he was, in the middle of the jungle, stepping from a helicopter as if he dropped in on them every day like that. They clustered round, and at once gossip was exchanged. Sam could not stay long; the engine could not be switched off, and soon it would run out of fuel. He quickly explained to these men that they would be returning to Tiwaeno when the road was completed to a certain stage. He switched from Wag to Spanish to Quichuan and even to English according to whom he was addressing. The Wagrani nodded trustingly.

'It's okay,' Sam told the oil official. 'They say they will go home, no problem. But they want to know what they will do for money in the future.'

That was something the oil company could not answer. They were relieved that the men had agreed with such ease. There is no doubt at all that the Wagrani are treated with the respect usually afforded to a dangerous wild beast, and at the same time they are treated as just another bunch of Indians. It is an uneasy combination and one can see that no one is quite sure about them. Sam is looked on as something of a mystery, an enigma. A real, wild Auca, who is better educated than many of the oil officials and who has friends in high places.

His job done, it was time to go to the Curaray.

21

Dayuma at Home in the Auca Protectorate

THE CLEARING WAS ALMOST DESERTED when the helicopter landed.
The lone figure of Dayuma was seen staring anxiously as the door opened.
When she saw Sam she tried hard to control her emotion, but the tears ran
down her cheeks.

Suddenly the place was filled with running figures talking excitedly, but
there was none of the spontaneous touching and holding there had been at
Cononaco. The children looked on with big eyes, or hung back warily. Only
Sam was accepted. The pilot and Señor Marcos of CEPE unloaded surprise
packages and boxes containing gifts for the Aucas contributed by all the workers
at Coca – clothes, pots, cookies, sweets, and mirrors and dolls for the girls, and
cars for the boys. The girls were not too keen on the dolls, which were pink
and plastic, but the boys soon tied twine to the cars and pulled them around.

There was an air of tension about the village due to their fear when they had
seen the helicopter. Rachel Saint's replacement, Patricia Kelly, had explained to
the group at Tiwaeno (who had passed it on to the group on the Curaray) on
one of her infrequent visits that the white man was angry when six workers
had recently been killed by Aucas. If it happened again, soldiers would come in
helicopters and machine-gun every Auca in the jungle.

'When we heard the helicopter,' Dayuma said, 'We were frightened. We
ran and hid in the jungle. Then I came out. Rachel had always told me to be an
example and to show no fear. God would take care of me.'

Sam was thoughtful. His original plan had been to ask the military to fly him
in. If he had gone in with the soldiers, who could tell what would have

happened? There were few men to be seen. He looked towards the trees. Were the men in the forest preparing to defend themselves?

The settlement on the Curaray is much more open and the houses much larger than those on the Cononaco which follow the traditional style. Many of them have separate sleeping quarters on stilts away from the eating and living hut. Dayuma slept on a mattress with mosquito net and blankets as did many of the others. Hammocks were used to sit on and rest. They were still made in the usual way by sticking two poles in the ground and weaving woven fibre string back and forth between them.

There was a small stream, that ran for about half a mile to the Curaray River through the village and extensive banana and yucca plantations. Ducks and geese swam and nested under upturned canoes below the raised houses. One day it rained a great deal and the stream overflowed. Ducks swam and children canoed right across the compound. The children played happily but more noisily together than the Cononaco children. They used pencil and paper, and made very good animals, aeroplanes and helicopters of clay.

When the children of Cononaco were given pencil and paper, they did not know what to do with them.

The people of Curaray were more withdrawn, more polite, if that is the correct word. They respected privacy and were less curious. They had even constructed toilets. One was a split-palm hut over a stream. The seat was an upturned canoe with a hole cut in it. There had not been a door, but one was made and hung after Sam's arrival. Another toilet was a deep pit in one half of a chicken house. This was near two houses where people lived who were crippled by polio. One of them was Sam's aunt, Enca. She was pale-faced with a gaunt and haggard look. She could walk a little but rested a great deal. Another cripple was a young man who could not walk at all. His wheelchair had been left in Tiwaeno when Dayuma's group of about fifty people moved to the Curaray. He had been carried across the difficult trail. He spent the day whittling wood and making excellent tools, an art which was foreign to their culture. Despite the fact that he could not move from his hammock, he had a sweet-faced wife who took good care of him and two small babies.

His father, also a polio victim, shared their house. He was the witch doctor Piyamo whose first son had been killed by Sam's teenage friends during the first few days of the introduction of the polio virus. He looked different from most of the other Wagrani; his face was larger and rounder and his hair was curly. He had a Buddha's stomach and wasted matchstick legs. He had once had a fight with a jaguar and had many scars to prove it. The jaguar had obviously not listened well to Piyamo who was supposed to have the power to converse

169

with these animals, especially the females.

Witch doctors are made, not born. Any child can be one. The parents merely have to go to a witch doctor immediately the child is born and tell him their desire. He is given certain herbs to drink and from then on must not eat certain food. And that is all there is to it. The benefits of being a witch doctor are dubious. He gets no payment, no rewards other than respect and, presumably, a *rapport* with the spirits and the animals. On the other hand, if anyone dies, it is because the witch doctor has cursed him, and sooner or later most witch doctors are speared. The witch doctor takes a drug, Aya huasca (*Banisteria Caapi*) which is made from the leaf of a bush and drunk like tea. It has a very powerful effect which, as Sam says, 'gives them quite a high'. But, also according to Sam, it is possible for a similar 'high' to be achieved through meditation. He has seen a witch doctor lying on his hammock, apparently in a complete trance, his mouth closed, and a deep voice, which is the witch doctor's own spirit, talking from his chest where a man's spirit lives until he dies and goes to heaven.

'The last time I saw this happen,' said Sam, 'Rachel got furious. She leaned over the guy and said "Are you the spirit of so and so, or are you the spirit of so and so?" She got no response. The man just carried on chanting away. Then she said, "I command you to be gone." When nothing happened she went off and got the gang together and they prayed for an hour or so.'

Sam described the subsequent events. The group at Tiwaeno had had a bad time hunting. For five days there had been no food, and Rachel was thinking about sending for some supplies to be flown in. The people had been eating bananas and yucca only. Even the fishing had been bad; barbarasco kills the fish in the river for weeks after it is used, and there were no fish to be had.

The witch doctor was consulted by the people. He went into a trance and spoke to the mother jaguar who told him where there was a whole herd of wild pig.

'So off they go, and sure enough they came back, with pig, a whole heap of them, enough to fill all the empty bellies. Okay, maybe it was coincidence, but it has happened many times. Now, the people saw that Rachel prayed – nothing. The witch doctor spoke and they had food. Naturally it's going to make them stick to the old ways.'

When Sam arrived in the helicopter Komi, Dayuma's husband, was not there. He had been away for several days hunting. Meat is not easy to come by in the Protectorate which has been over-hunted for many years, but this time he had had a good trip. There were several wild pig. He had carried one weighing about seventy pounds for many hours through the jungle at night and had not lost his way. The pig was cut up in the stream by Dayuma's daughters, and divided between the various families, Dayuma keeping the best part for her own family.

Today her family consists of Nancy, Eva, and Solomon. She had another daughter, Eunie, who was born with tumours in both eyes. At one time, a child such as Eunie would have been thrown away, but Eunie had both eyes removed and lived until she was seven, when she was accidentally drowned while playing. Rachel Saint had been particularly fond of Eunie.

The people in Curaray are warm and generous, and Dayuma treated her white guests with great consideration. Clothes were washed, food prepared, and special treats of jungle fruit provided. Everything was done with less exuberance than on the Cononaco, but nevertheless with as much thoughtfulness. The people all wear clothes, even to bathe in, which looks very odd as they soap themselves under their shirts and below their dresses. The girls also swim in their clothes as a matter of form, even when they expect to be alone. They are strong, powerful swimmers, but the clothes must hamper them.

Shoes are worn by most adults, but not by the children, whose feet take on the customary Wagrani shape of strong, splayed toes. The pain when those feet are later jammed into tight, modern, plastic shoes must be considerable, but they do not seem to notice it. The women also wear what can only be described as fancy pants. Washing lines were decorated with frilly nylon undies in delicate pastel shades. Cystitis and athlete's foot are inevitable under these circumstances. One of the recently airlifted Ridge group was there. He was the only man to remove all his hampering and hot clothes when he was working chopping down a tree. He did it with a total lack of self-consciousness, although Komi and Dayuma looked most embarrassed.

'We are frightened to take them off,' was Dayuma's simple answer when asked why her people wear clothes when obviously they are not necessary at all times. She did not enlarge on what they were afraid of – she could have meant 'shy', but there is no such word in Wag.

She was asked what good things had happened since the missionaries came in to teach them.

'Now I know the truth about God. I know he is my friend, and I like to be able to pray to him when I have many problems and need help. It is good also that we love our children and do not kill each other. But that is all. I do not like anything else. They make us pay for medicine when we have no money. They sell us old clothes. They do not keep their promises, and now they have taken Rachel away and she is not allowed to return.'

One of the reasons why they were so concerned over medicine was that a cold epidemic had spread through their ranks, and unable to cope with it, several people were quite ill. Only the week before Sam's arrival, a woman had died, and another had been buried the previous day, and several children were sick. They had no antibiotics left, and had reported all this on the radio to Limoncocha. Dayuma asked to speak in Quichuan to the pilot, whom she held in special regard. He was embarrassed and replied that he had been given his instructions – 'No medicine unless it is paid for in advance.'

'I hope no more people die,' was Dayuma's response.

Dayuma moved to the Curaray from Tiwaeno after Rachel left because she did not like the replacements who, she said, came for an hour or two to check them over, and then left: 'We do not like to be watched.'

She was very anxious for news of Rachel Saint and listened carefully as Sam explained that Rachel had been ill, in America, but was now well, and living in Quito.

'Why does she live in that cold city when she can live here, in her own house?' Dayuma asked.

'Because when she is here, in the jungle, she does not do her work. She must finish God's carving,' Sam explained.

'Why can't she finish it here?' Dayuma asked. 'I was helping her before. Doesn't she want me to help her any more?'

Sam tried to explain that it was not as simple as that. Her superiors in the SIL thought that Rachel Saint was getting too emotionally involved with the Wagrani and was not doing her main translating work efficiently. Dayuma did not understand, although she looked at Sam with her wide, brown eyes as he explained. She smiled slightly, as if to say, 'What nonsense!'

'And you, Sam? How are you? I was told you might be abroad, or you might be dead.'

Then the story that Dayuma had been told when she wanted news of Sam was related, and it was Sam's turn to be rather surprised. He said little, but assured his mother that many of the things she had been told about him were not true.

'We have been told that you have rejected us. That you have told the newspapers in Quito many bad things about us,' Dayuma said.

The people crowded around as the discussion moved backwards and forwards until all were satisfied about the facts. Dayuma asked about Christina.

'Bring her here,' she told Sam. 'I am looking forward to meeting her.'

'I was told that you were angry with her,' Sam said.

'No, why should I be?' Dayuma was surprised and upset. Later she gave Sam gifts to take back to Christina.

Throughout the days that followed, it could be seen that Dayuma's chief concern was Rachel Saint. She talked about her constantly and could not understand why Rachel had gone away apparently never to return. She could not understand why she had sent no message, had not spoken on the radio, had not been able to see Dayuma when she had made the long journey to Quito.

'People cannot always do as they want,' Sam said. 'Although they may try.'

Dayuma decided that Sam should go at once to see if Rachel's house was still in good shape. Rachel had, in fact, sent a message with Sam asking Dayuma to pack away some of her favourite clothes – a warm wool poncho, some frocks, some good shoes – she had not expected to be away so long and had left them hanging up in her house in Tiwaeno. Dayuma did not want to make the trip to Tiwaeno; there was still sickness at Curaray and she might be needed.

Sam left for Tiwaeno at dawn, accompanied by some of the bachelors who had nothing better to do and his white friends. He took gifts of rice and biscuits for his grandmother, old Akawo.

The Curaray settlement is a few yards from Palm Beach where the five missionaries died. Today nothing remains of that sandbank but a small area of pebbles worn smooth by centuries of time. Water laps in ochre swirls where once the small yellow aeroplane swooped down upon firm sand. Memories of their last meal of hot blueberry muffins and ice-cream seem bizarre in that setting. Tall bamboo lines the clay banks, a solid wall. Nothing can be seen of the place where five men lie buried.

The Indian gestured. 'There,' he said. 'Beyond the bamboo, under the ciba tree, that is where they are.'

There was nothing to tell what thoughts ran through his head as he looked towards the wide-spreading canopy of the ciba tree. He had helped kill the five Americans in his youth, and can't remember how many others he had killed over the years.

Now he wears clothes, a brown paper hat, and lives in peace just around the river bend.

Travelling upriver in long dugout canoes is slow, against the current. The Wagrani Indians use simple poles of bamboo, cut fresh each trip with casual swipes of their machetes. They pole by pushing into the mud of the river bed, one man in the prow and one in the stern, balancing easily. The shallow river is full of hazards; hidden banks and great trees swept from mountain slopes in lightning storms and landslides. Landslides are frequent, particularly where the endless sea of the Amazon jungle meets the ridges and slopes of the Andean foothills. The fragile hold that such a vast army of trees, such an endless carpet of ferns and creepers and bushes has on the thin soil can clearly be seen at the site of the slips. Red earth over yellow clay is exposed, raw and naked, and roots, snaking in shallow parallel lines, like the legs of myriapodic spiders, unable to dig down and maintain a firm grip on the land.

The river was low, and long, sandy banks merged with the faded colour of the water in the dawn light. Small tendrils of mist swirled through the reeds and bamboo and now and then a distant tree on the opposite hill suddenly appeared, hanging in the air, as the cloudy vapour shifted.

The evening before, the girls of the tribe had run through the shallows, lifting their skirts over sturdy, brown legs, laughing as they sprawled with the fat babies they carried into the cool pools. The evening sun had spread a golden glow, dazzling in all the reflections.

Now in the first light the water was silver and dim.

Some of the large trees lying prone in the river were arched, the arches covered with hanging moss, vivid green-tongued fern and pale green sprouts of grass, making a frame to outline darker pools and the distant bank.

The mist began to lift, moving in clinging pockets from the trees, and the distant hills began to take shape. Some of them were very steep, and, outlined down the slopes, lines of palm were seen, black against the clouds, stark silhouettes from tropical islands. Flowering plants appeared in batches; blue and white convolvulus, leaves as large as saucers, almost hanging in the water; a flame-red tree, a dark-yellow one, and a bush covered with pale yellow flowers. Most of them were too distant to identify. Round another bend, and there was a tall tree, silver grey trunk, hanging with purple flowers, like the bloom on a great, round grape. It was delicious and voluptuous and all too quickly gone.

In the middle of the river, on a grey arch of a submerged tree was a row of grey and yellow birds.

'Flycatchers,' Sam said.

The birds flashed across the bow of the canoe, their bright yellow feathers brilliant against the grey water. From the opposite bank came two blue and white heron and for a moment it seemed that their paths would collide. The heron flew steadily, with a calm, lazy flap of spread-feather wings, and the flycatchers flew up over them in a series of small swoops, to fan out as they reached the reeds, little yellow and grey jewels, hanging over the water on separate leaves.

The men stopped the canoe for a moment and it drifted back slightly until a pole was pushed into the mud, and it held, water making a musical ripple against the new angle of the canoe and the pole. A large cream and brown hawk sat in the branches of a thorn tree and stared silently back at them. All was still and quiet, but for the sound of the water.

The smell was the earthy, reedy smell of water and mud; the deep, intense smell that seems to hold time in its odour. A shift of the light morning breeze, and there was wood smoke, sharp and dangerous. The men appeared not to heed it, and started to pole against the current as the hawk flew into an even taller tree upriver. The canoe kept pace with it; as it flew upriver, the canoe went too, until, shrugging off boring humans, the great beautiful bird flew up and up, to a distant high hill.

'There he is,' Sam said, nodding. 'In that tree next to that toucan.' There was nothing to see; just a far, black tree outlined against the sky.

'In a moment, the toucan will fly,' Sam said.

And in a moment, the toucan, a small, dark speck, did fly towards the river, and soon his brilliant colours and large beak were clearly seen.

All the Indians seem to have the most astonishing sense of sight, of hearing and of smell. City people discover that, after a few weeks in the jungle, they too develop a quickening of the senses. Although Sam spends much of his time in Quito these days and has travelled widely, he has not lost the instincts for survival that he learnt in the jungle. Even in Quito he seems to have an uncanny telepathic ability – which is based on a heightened sense of awareness rather than on any claims based on extra-sensory perception.

The smell of wood smoke grew stronger, and round the next bend of the river was a small settlement of two long, elliptical palm thatch Wagrani huts.

Twenty years ago no group of travelling Wagrani would pass a Wagrani settlement without a certain amount of apprehension. A Wagrani's greatest enemy used to be another Wagrani.

The family in the huts were eating their morning meal, and they stared politely at the strangers in the canoe, but said nothing, not even to their relative Sam, whom they had not seen for over two years.

'That is the home of Kimo,' Sam said. 'He was one who killed those five missionaries back in 1956.'

The miles passed and the sun rose higher, although never entirely breaking through the cloud cover. The colours of the trees, of the hills, of the water, were changing all the time. The water was a particularly beautiful combination of a clear green and violet, like an aquarelle, and unlike its more usual Amazon mustard.

At noon, the canoe arrived at a path hidden by overhanging shrubs. The Wagrani stopped and tied the canoe with a long rope. There would be plenty of rain in the night, and the river would rise. The canoe needed a long line. Then they had a small meal of hard-boiled eggs, brought from the outside by Sam, and they drank the unfermented yucca drink called *chicha* which is carried as a thick, cooked paste, and diluted by river water. It tastes like yogurt and has the texture of mashed pineapple.

A stranger travelling by river would not see the path from the Curaray River across the ridge to the Tiwaeno River. The men stepped from the canoe, bending under an overhanging branch, then plunged straight up a steep clay trail. At once the track was evident, and with machetes they cut recent growth as they travelled. The air was hot and still, and the plants were bright green, almost startling in their richness and texture. Fat, crisp orchids hung down on trailing vines, pink and orange. Brilliant vermillion flowers, like the crest on a bird, opened up to the shafts of sun. Sounds were closer, more solid. On the river, the calls of the birds had echoed like bells across the valley, sweet and sharp. In the forest the sounds were less clear, everything seemingly blotted out by the drone, the chatter and the buzz of the insects. They were well-mannered insects; they kept themselves to themselves, and not once bothered the party of very hot travellers.

The trail went through thick loam, through dark bogs, traversed by cut trees, over sparkling, gravel-bottomed streams, and up a hill that seemed never to end. Steps formed by exposed roots of the soaring trees led the way up the forty-five degree slope. At times the distant river could be seen, and at times the trail was on a narrow ridge, scarcely a metre wide, as the slope fell steeply away on both sides.

The Wagrani travelled in tight-fitting shoes and old, torn jeans. Sam walked barefoot, his strong toes gripping roots and helping. He wore shorts and looked cool and comfortable. The men found the trousers clinging to their legs in the damp heat, but still they retained them.

The leader stopped and pointed to the clay on the trail; large jaguar prints, recently made, going in their direction. They moved on. Soon they stopped again, and examined more prints, telling the story of the wild boar hunt of the previous day. Five boar had been killed, three speared and two shot, and the meat had been carried in the dark, downriver to the settlement where Dayuma, Sam's mother, lived, and they all had feasted well.

The slope fell away, the path lined by an endless border of little red flowers pointing the way to Tiwaeno. The first house was soon seen, on the opposite side of the Tiwaeno River, and higher than the main settlement. With the sight came the smell of a village; the bark of a dog, and amazingly, the lowing of cattle. The missionaries had introduced the cattle. Since the missionaries' coming, the people are now largely settled; it was their nomadic way of life,

A former killer and 'witch doctor' from the dangerous Ridge area, taken into the Protectorate by missionary intervention. Not used to clothes yet, he takes them off to work – embarrassing some of his new group

ABOVE: Vital to Ecador's economy, oil wells are having a drastic effect on Wagrani territory, though oil men are as considerate as possible. BOTTOM LEFT: Sam tries to persuade Wagrani, who were offered work through missionary instigation, to return home. Only Sam, who is multi-lingual, understands both sides

following game, that gave them food. Now, food must come to them.

The forest was left, and there was Tiwaeno, dominated by a long, grassy airstrip, like a well-trimmed lawn.

There were white Brahmin cattle, farmyard fowl, a generator. A disused church hut stood by the sparkling river, thick grass growing where once was beaten earth. The people were warm and welcoming and Sam's grandmother, the old women, Akawo, came in a faded cotton overall, leaning on a tall stick, and holding the hand of her friend, an even older woman, dressed in a very dirty man's tee-shirt. They had no teeth, and waited for biscuits dunked in sweet tea as their special treat.

Akawo seemed as old as Time itself. Her face was wrinkled and she was toothless. Her toes were so splayed that her big toe pointed nearly backwards. Her skin was grimy, her hair unkempt, and her faded pink dress was more black than pastel. But she radiated a welcome, affection for Sam, and interest in his friends. Her expression was so vivid and mobile that here, one felt, was a real character. Certainly, she had a wicked sense of humour. One could imagine her on a doorstep in Cockney London or in a French farmhouse, doling out herbal remedies and scandal. Dayuma had the same dry sense of humour as Sam, a very sweet expression, and gentle ways. Akawo, one felt, was a roguish old lady. There was an obvious deep *rapport* between her and Sam.

It was not possible to get into Rachel's house; the door was too firmly locked and none of the keys fitted.

Sam and the men bathed in the river; Sam was the only one to strip. The men who had come with him from the Curaray seemed shy and retained their clothes in the water. They walked back from the river, and their feet, released from the tightly fitting shoes, were broad, toes spreading out, used from childhood to grip slippery slopes as they ran through the jungle. They were not to be free for long. The young men had carried a change of clothes with them; vivid-coloured flared leg trousers, tightly moulded to hip and buttock, and floral shirts. Platform soled shoes were found, and thus elegantly attired, the two young men swanned around the village, eyeing the girls very casually and chatting to their fellow bachelors, who soon disappeared into their own houses, to re-emerge similarly clad. There was a regular fashion parade of young bloods up and down the airstrip, while Sam, the much-travelled young man, relaxed in his torn cut-aways and bare feet on the steps of his mother's former house and talked to his grandmother.

Rachel Saint's house stands on the banks of the Tiwaeno River, next to Dayuma's house. It is surrounded by a hedge of bright pink flowers, like the

TOP: Two cultures met in Tiwaeno – Rachel and Elisabeth Elliot grew very close to Wagrani women, Rachel closest of all to Dayuma (third from left) – but (BELOW) today, Rachel's house stands empty. Outside, symbolically, pink flower cuttings from Nate Saint's house at Shell Mera where he flew from to his death

feathery crests of crowned crane. It is empty; there is no one there.

Dayuma's house in Tiwaeno is big. It is built on stilts off the ground, and has many rooms, divided by bamboo walls and doors. The outside walls are filled in with mosquito netting, not to keep the insects away, but to keep out the vampire bats, which lap up the blood of their victims at night.

Dayuma's house was filled with the most remarkable furniture, in strong contrast to the more simple materials she had at the Curaray, and one wondered where it had come from and how it had got here. There was a double bed with a solid carved headboard, marble-topped tables, a surgical couch, a gas stove, a double sink and drainer, chests of drawers, shelves of stores, tables, beds, chairs. Surely all these things had not been flown in from Quito in a small, light aircraft? But remembering a solid cast-iron sewing-machine table, weighing over two hundred pounds, carried on Komi's back across the jungle trail and downriver to the Curaray settlement I shouldn't have been surprised at anything.

The people of Tiwaeno were, if anything, more shy and nervous than those on the Curaray. Several people airlifted from the Ridge were there, and they seemed to be apart from the others. There was apparently no unpleasantness, but these people did seem uneasy, almost lost.

Sam verified this impression. 'They want to go to Cononaco,' he said. 'I'm going to ask Captain Flores to fly here, then take them. I can afford two trips, then I will have to save up again to take more.'

Sam said their chief problem was the lack of game. The newcomers had not been there long enough to have *chacras* of their own, and food had been a real problem with them. They had gone hungry at times, for although the Christian Indians at Tiwaeno had shared generously, they could not do so all the time when they had little enough of their own. One of the reasons why Dayuma had left was to go to the good crops on the Curaray.

'These people were airlifted in, then left here,' Sam said. 'It was not very fair in my opinion to leave them without food.'

Sam had reason to be concerned. On his limited resources, single-handed, without substantial help from charities and collecting-boxes in the States, he had been helping to support a large group on the Cononaco. One could see why he felt that the same support should be given in Tiwaeno, despite the SIL's natural wish not to 'spoil' the people or make them over-dependent.

'These people should be assisted for a while,' Sam said.

'They are not here through choice, therefore the responsibility for survival is not entirely theirs.'

When Sam left Tiwaeno, a few members of the new Ridge group accompanied him back to the Curaray. No visits had been made to the riverside settlements on the way west upriver to Tiwaeno, but on the easier return trip, visits were made, and Sam stopped to drink *chicha* with old friends. He met again the old Záparo woman, remembered from his childhood on the hacienda of Don Carlos Sevilla. She was very like Akawo in features and in manner. She cackled with laughter and played tricks, seemingly very entertained by Sam's friends. She cooked whole sweetcorn in the fire, handing them around. They were hot and tender when the husks had been peeled back, and tasted far superior to the more usual Western boiled-out-of-their-skin method. Smoking over the fire were the feet of a deer and the remaining meat inside the shell of a big green turtle. The villages were large, far larger than could be seen from the river, extending far back into the forest.

'You can see how many Wagrani are here in the Protectorate,' Sam said. 'And you can, perhaps, understand some of the hunting problems. Game doesn't hang around to be killed. They can smell people, and move off.'

The truth in what he says is borne out by the abundance of game on the Cononaco. Sam is fighting to get a larger Protectorate zone, and he has an ally in Padre Labaca, a Capuchin monk on the Napo, but the land that is needed is considerably larger than the area allocated. Sam thinks it will take a great deal to convince the government of his people's needs. Both he and Padre Labaca think the Wagrani can manage on nothing less than the whole of their original territory.

'Maybe when all the oil has run out and the settlers have given up after their naked soil has blown away in the wind; maybe then, when no one wants the land, the people can have it back,' Sam said with a slight smile.

Ranchers in Texas who found oil on their land became millionaires overnight – conversely, Aucas who have oil on their land find themselves in a worse position economically. These people have simple tastes. They do not want vast wealth, they merely want those two most basic human rights: sufficient food to hunt and grow – and freedom. Not much to ask, one would think.

Dayuma herself is the first to admit now that the Protectorate has proved to be too small. One cannot blame her; after all, in her educational background what had there been to teach her how much land *per capita* was the basic requirement of a Wagrani?

A bee-hive hunt for honey was organized on Sam's return. It was conducted with the air of a fiesta. Small boys galloping about in new, brightly-coloured shorts – the gift of CEPE – dived into bushes with little regard for all the dangers that would terrify a Westerner; snakes, scorpions, thorns. They cut thin, green stalks and used them as spears, aiming them at each other until they decided that one of the young men would make a good quarry and they pursued him through the thick undergrowth, falling on him *en masse* in wild screams of laughter.

While this game was in progress, a huge bee-hive was found, about forty feet up a thick tree, hanging from the first spreading bough. It was grey and smooth, shaped like an American football and about six feet long.

Reaching it was rather drastic. The tree was chopped down. The men judged almost to an inch where to fell the tree. A foot in either direction and the hive would have been lost; the tree would have merely keeled over to rest against another monster beside it in the close-packed jungle growth. The minute the tree was down the men dived into the nest, broke off a piece of the comb, then ran, the honey dripping through their fingers, their heads and bodies smothered in the small, dark sweat bees. The honey was consumed at once with wide smiles and appreciative gurgles and sucks. The path back to the village was sticky, littered with broken bits of the comb, which was endless in quantity. A six-foot hive is quite substantial. Some bits were taken back to Dayuma and her daughters.

Dayuma sat placidly in her eating house (she has two houses – an enclosed one on stilts where she sleeps and one, simply a roof, constructed on the bare earth for cooking and eating). She took the comb pieces in a large, dug-out wooden dish, her eyes sparkling in secret laughter, as if to say to Sam and the young men, 'You're crazy, all of you!'

Dayuma commands an enormous amount of respect and there is no doubt at all that she is in charge. Her husband is a quiet and handsome consort, who follows Dayuma's every word, every gesture, with devotion; but he is far from doglike. He is a strong man, and although he keeps in the background, it is also obvious that Dayuma depends on him. Each evening they sat in their hammock near the fire, swinging in the reflected light while they told stories, a contented, devoted couple after nearly twenty years.

During the day, Dayuma conducts activities, discussing the building of the new school, of the projected airstrip – even of the football pitch, which is where the helicopter was able to land.

Football is of great interest to these Wagrani and one even produced a transistor radio in order to follow the World Cup Final in Argentina. How they knew the Cup Final was in progress, or even what it meant, was a mystery. The Spanish commentary was translated into Wag by the educated young man who had been taught to write and read in Limoncocha during his period as a polio victim. Dayuma hopes he will be as useful a teacher as Toña was.

She was asked if she thought education was important so that the Wagrani could be integrated into the Ecuadorian society of Quito, but she shook her head.

'No, my people do not want to live anywhere else but in the jungle.' She said she herself would never leave the jungle. Quito was cold and noisy. This was her father's land, and it was her land. She loved it more than any other place she had ever seen. But education was important. It helped people understand things – it helped them even in their life in the jungle, and it was good to understand things.

The two girls, Sam's sisters, were asked if they wanted to go to school in Quito as Sam had done – perhaps even go to college in America. They smiled shyly and shook their heads. Eventually they confessed that they were nervous of being eaten by the white man. Eaten perhaps by mistake, they said, but by then it would be too late.

Dayuma has not taught them this – it is a part of the tribe's legend, and seemingly hard to erase. Not surprisingly, since it is one of the Wagrani mothers' favourite punishments for their children in Tiwaeno and on the Curaray, according to Sam, to threaten their children with white horrors.

'I guess they think it toughens them up,' Sam said. Dayuma had treated him in exactly the same way when he was a child. 'But I don't think she did it to the others after she met Rachel,' he said.

Although Rachel Saint is not there and has never been to the Curaray settlement, she is there in spirit: in the Sunday service Dayuma holds, in the clothes the people wear, in the way Dayuma is teacher and nurse, in the modesty of the people, in the single marriage unions, in the projected new school, in the simple Wagrani-Spanish story books and New Testament translation lying about on the floor of Dayuma's house.

These people are very different from the Cononaco group, but it is not possible to say whether they are better or worse; happier or less happy. They are shyer and less responsive, so their feelings are difficult to judge. They are as good-natured and as generous and certainly less demanding. They gave freely of everything and touched nothing that was not theirs. They had more in the way of material goods and possessions except for that one vital element – food. They had banana, plantain, maize and yucca in abundance. There were domestic fowl – but there was less game, less fish, and these people do depend on meat protein in their daily diet.

One hunter returned from a long hunting trip with his family. He had taken them with him, including a newly-born baby, because he knew he would be away a week. The women in the group carried baskets full of smoked whole monkey, looking like sooty devils. The image was sharpened by a small and anxious live baby monkey, clinging pathetically to his dead mother's smoked hand.

They were going to keep it for a pet until they decided that it was too young to rear, so the children were given their junior-sized blowguns and allowed to use the pathetic, big-eyed creature as target practice. It hid in the rafters of their hut and squealed.

'It will soon be over,' Sam said. 'Don't be too upset.'

Riddled like a pincushion, the little monkey eventually did die, but it was difficult not to feel upset. This had been no different to the treatment meted out to a small long-eared mouse on the banks of the Cononaco. But it seemed worse because the monkey looked so like a human baby.

Sometimes during the evenings Dayuma talked of Rachel and of her visit to the United States. She looked with interest at the photographs in her book *The Dayuma Story*, pointing out to the people clustered about her such details as a skyscraper or an enormous aeroplane. She attempted to describe, with sounds and expression, with eloquent gestures, what the pictures represented. Dayuma is an excellent narrator. It was quite possible to know what she was talking about by her talented mimes. Her story-telling is even more fascinating, and she certainly is the equivalent of the wandering minstrel of Europe in the eyes of the people.

Dayuma last saw Rachel Saint 'about two chonta seasons ago' – that is, about one year and five months, and she said she had no idea when she could expect to see her again. 'Her bosses won't let her come back,' she said, simply.

She talked of the deep friendship and love she and Rachel had built up between themselves over the years. They were as sisters and Rachel was now a part of her family. Even though Rachel had no husband, she did not need to fear the future, they would take care of her.

'Rachel wanted to get married once, when she was quite young,' Dayuma said. 'She made many plans. But,' laughing, 'he married someone else. Young men are like that. Can never see what is valuable. So then she said she would never marry anyone. She would work just for God.'

She added that even if Rachel had not told her all the truths about God, she would still love her. 'She is a good person,' she explained.

Dayuma does not think very much of some other 'good people' who have forced them into a situation where their men must walk to Mishuali or Tena (in the foothills of the Andes) in order to trade their hammocks, blowguns and other of their few traditional items for a small sum.

'We even have to buy old and torn clothes. I know that these are gifts to the missionaries at Limoncocha, because Rachel has told me they are often given by friends. Why then must we pay?'

There seems no answer – certainly the accusations were denied by the missionaries at Limoncocha. So one must either believe Dayuma or not.

Dayuma's opinion about men who have more than one wife is rather enigmatic. 'Some men have five,' she said and laughed with real amusement, but she would not be drawn on whether it was right or wrong.

She herself would not want even two. Komi was a fine husband and no other husband or husbands would be as good as he.

Dayuma has only one ambition, apart from hoping that she will see Rachel again. She wants enough money to be able to buy medicine when it is required, to buy some cattle and some pigs and to be able to go to the dentist when necessary. The bad teeth that afflict her people is a great trial to Dayuma, particularly after seeing the strong, healthy teeth of outsiders. She wants better for the Wagrani and understands that research may give some of the answers, but for that and to pay for the dental scientists, money is needed.

'If my people have enough food, good health, strong teeth, and some education, they will need nothing else.'

Such a prayer has been offered even by the richest man when he is tired and mortally sick.

Dayuma thinks that if Rachel is not well she should return to the jungle. After her own experience in North America, she is not prepared to accept that anyone is better off living there if they are ill.

'Rachel Saint should come back here,' Sam said. 'It's what she wants to do. What's holding her back? She should forget about religion and just concentrate on God. There's no point in spending her whole life translating the Bible into a language no one can read. These people are like children and can be taught truths. They pass them down in their traditions, and that means a lot more than a pile of paper which the termites will eat.

'They say "dust to dust". What relevance can the history of Israel possibly have in the jungle? Christ never wrote one single recorded word in his whole life. When he did write once, it was on the sand of the sea-shore, and the wind blew the words away. But his truth survives. That is how it will be here. If Rachel has taught truths, they will survive.'

'Tell her to come,' Dayuma said. 'She is my sister and I miss her. She has no husband but we will repair her house and we will feed her and Komi will hunt for her. Tell her to come. This is her home and we are waiting.'